STUDY STRATEGIES PLUS

Building Your Study Skills and Executive Functioning for School Success

by

Sandi Sirotowitz, M.Ed.
Leslie Davis, M.Ed.
Harvey C. Parker, Ph.D.

Specialty Press, Inc.
Plantation, Florida
(800) 233-9273

Illustrations by Richard Dimatteo
Cover Design and Book Layout by Kall Graphics, Inc.
Edited by Dara K. Levan

Specialty Press, Inc.
300 Northwest 70th Ave, Suite 102
Plantation, Florida 33317
(954) 792-8100 • (800) 233-9273
www.addwarehouse.com

Printed in the United States of America
ISBN-10   1-886949-11-5
ISBN-13   9781886949119

DEDICATION

We dedicate this book to our wonderful grandchildren
Taylor, Jordyn, Caian, Jaelyn, Hartley, and Halle
with love beyond measure.
You are the future—bright with promise.

What others are saying about *Study Strategies Plus*

The authors of *Study Strategies Plus* have hit another home run! As a principal of a private school with a challenging academic program, I am always searching for the best current practices to offer our teachers and students. When we incorporated strategies from *Study Strategies Made Easy* into our middle and high school curriculum, teachers reported dramatic improvements in students' performances. With its expanded content, such as executive functioning, *Study Strategies Plus* produces even greater results.

— *Gayle Iacono, Principal, Sagemont Upper School, Weston, FL*

Study Strategies Plus has been the best resource for teaching my incoming college freshmen how to prepare and study. It is filled with activities that are practical, student-friendly and easily generalized into many of their courses. My students report that by using this workbook, they are becoming more organized and prepared for the rigors of college.

— *Bryna Siegel Finer, Ph.D., English Professor, Pittsburgh, PA.*

When my learning center was offered the opportunity to pilot *Study Strategies Plus* with our students, I carefully researched its contents and decided to participate. Parents, teachers, tutors and especially our middle and high school students as well as entering college freshmen are thrilled with the results. Our students went from being dependent on help from their parents and tutors to being organized, active students now able to rely upon their own efficient skills. Based upon the overwhelmingly positive results, *Study Strategies Plus* is an integral resource for all of our students.

— *Jill Rickel, Owner/Certified Educational Planner, Academic Options, Weston, FL*

My students are hearing impaired and have many of the same learning issues that hearing students do. I was gratified to find that I could adapt *Study Strategies Plus* to meet the needs of my students and was thrilled with the results.

— *Elizabeth Davis, teacher, Santa Barbara, CA*

TABLE OF CONTENTS

PREFACE— A NOTE TO STUDENTS, TEACHERS, AND PARENTS

A Note to Students

The title of this book is *Study Strategies Plus*. The purpose of our first book, *Study Strategies Made Easy,* was to introduce methods that would teach students *how* to learn. We were gratified from the feedback we received. Thousands of students, teachers, and parents saw positive results when they used our strategies.

Over the next few years, education and educational research matured to open up new avenues of understanding in the learning process. One of these is that how we learn is intimately linked to how well we are able to understand, monitor, and adapt our responses to our environment. The term for this is "executive functioning." As we learned more about this area, we began to add strategies for executive functioning to our *Study Strategies Made Easy,* which is the "Plus" in *Study Strategies Plus*.

In this book, there are chapters that define executive functions and the strategies that are relative to those functions. In addition, we included the specific learning strategies that proved so effective in *Study Strategies Made Easy*. In both books, we utilize the results of the most current educational research. When students are taught how to apply these strategies, they can become consciously proficient and make their school experiences more productive and meaningful.

If we tell a child what to think, we make him a slave to our knowledge. If we teach a child how to think, we make all knowledge his slave. That was our mantra in *Study Strategies Made Easy* and *Study Strategies for Early School Success* and it is again our guiding belief in *Study Strategies Plus*.

How to use Study Strategies Plus

1. Complete the Checklist of Skills in chapter one. You will be able to see which study strategies you already use and any that you need to modify or add to become the best student you can be.

2. From the information you derive from the checklist, you can choose to follow each chapter sequentially or you can first read and follow the chapters that most strongly relate to your own needs. In either case, even if you think you already do what you should be doing, you will find ways to refine and improve what you do for even better ways to school success.

3. Read the stories at the beginning of each chapter about students who are experiencing learning and study issues that you may find similar to your own. Then learn the strategies and apply them to your own work.

4. Do the activities that are in the book and then apply them to your schoolwork using your own materials. The only way to make these strategies work for you is to practice them consistently. Think of the athlete who practices one play for a whole season just to get his mind and body to know it automatically. Professional musicians also practice the same piece every day for hours. You, the student, want to get your study skills on autopilot in the same way as the athlete or musician.

5. Complete the final Checklist of Skills in the last chapter so you can chart the progress you have made since starting to apply the strategies from *Study Strategies Plus*.

A Note to Teachers

> "Once the classroom door closes, once the lesson begins,
> once the student steps toward the teacher asking for help,
> it is all up to the teacher, not the school.
> Good schools help; great schools help more;
> but great teachers are the far more precious commodity."
>
> —Temes

We are delighted that research has proven what students and teachers have always known—teachers make the difference! We recall specific teachers for a lifetime; some with great fondness and if we are lucky, one or two with the understanding that they changed the course of our lives. It is for that reason that we are indebted to great teachers who teach strategies and techniques that have a positive impact their students' lives.

Study Strategies Plus is addressed to students. However, we believe that the best method for students to learn and apply these strategies for long-term results is with the guidance of teachers or study coaches. Therefore, as you read through the book, you will see that all strategies and activities are designed to be used with large or small groups as well as individuals. They are beneficial for middle, high school and even beginning college students.

Some suggestions for teachers and study coaches:

- Teach a "strategy of the week" using both verbal and visual directions. Review the new strategy during the week and ask students how they are beginning to incorporate it into their studying. Encourage students to think metacognitively as they apply the strategies to their unique learning situations.

- Provide a visual aid, perhaps a poster on a "strategy wall" or a PowerPoint® shown at intervals in your classroom. This will allow students to refer to the strategies as they are learning them.

- Model the practice activities, so that your students can "watch" and "listen" to how you think.

- Scaffold your lessons, using the practice activities in the book, until you are sure that your students have internalized strategies and are ready to generalize them to the content you are teaching.

- Provide time for students to practice applying the strategies you taught. Students can do this via pair-share, cooperative learning, and reciprocal teaching. They will need consistency and time to make the use of these strategies a habitual part of their study routine.

- We recognize that in the beginning this will take extra time in your already over scheduled day. However, the payoff for you and your students will be worth it.

A Note to Parents

The best gift you can give your child is to provide him or her with the tools to become independent, efficient, motivated, and ultimately a successful student. We hope that *Study Strategies Plus* will help you achieve this.

Chapter One

WHAT ARE YOU DOING NOW?

A QUESTIONNAIRE OF EXECUTIVE FUNCTIONING AND STUDY STRATEGIES

You will learn new and more efficient ways of studying using *Study Strategies Plus*. Before you begin, take a few minutes to evaluate your present skills.

Directions: Read each question below. If you almost always do what is asked, write "Y." If you almost never do what is asked, write "N." If you sometimes do what is asked, though not enough, write "S." Then add up all of your "Y" responses and write the total number of those to get your Study Skills Rating.

ORGANIZATION

_____ 1. Do I have a neat, organized place to do my homework?

_____ 2. Do I have good organizing habits and organize regularly?

_____ 3. Do I keep my notebooks and materials organized so I can easily find what I need?

_____ 4. Do I frequently keep track of my grades?

TIME MANAGEMENT

_____ 5. Do I have a good sense of time so that I can estimate how long an assignment should take me?

_____ 6. Do I write down a time schedule of homework, study, and activities?

_____ 7. Do I budget my time so I get everything done within the required time limits?

_____ 8. Do I assess how my time budget went and plan changes if necessary?

STARTING, FOCUSING, AND FINISHING

_____ 9. Do I start assignments without procrastinating?

_____ 10. Do I stick with assignments until they are completed?

_____ 11. Do I delay what is fun to work on an assignment that is required?

_____ 12. Do I complete and turn in my assignments on time?

PLANNING AND PRIORITIZING

_____ 13. Do I plan how to get my homework and studying done?

_____ 14. Do I follow a written action plan for getting work done?

_____ 15. Do I prioritize the work I need to do?

_____ 16. Do I make and follow a written plan to complete long-term assignments?

SELF-MONITORING AND METACOGNITION

_____ 17. Do I think about which learning style and strategies to use for a task?

_____ 18. Do I have a plan before starting an assignment?

_____ 19. Do I monitor how I'm doing and make changes if I need to?

_____ 20. Do I evaluate how I did and plan changes I might make for the next assignment?

LEARNING STYLES

_____ 21. Do I know my preferred learning style(s)?

_____ 22. Do I use my best styles of learning when I study?

_____ 23. Do I know in what environment I study best?

COMMUNICATION

_____ 24. Do I think that my teachers usually see my behaviors as positive?

_____ 25. Do I usually know what each teacher expects of me?

_____ 26. Do I know how to ask for help from teachers when I need it?

READING COMPREHENSION

_____ 27. Do I think about and pay attention to what I am reading?

_____ 28. Can I identify topics, main ideas, and supporting details in a reading selection?

_____ 29. Do I paraphrase what I read?

_____ 30. Do I use signal words to help me identify important information in my textbooks?

_____ 31. Do I preview textbook chapters?

_____ 32. Do I have successful methods to learn and retain new vocabulary?

SUMMARIZING AND NOTE TAKING

_____ 33. Do I summarize information from readings and lectures?

_____ 34. Do I know different ways to take notes?

_____ 35. Do I take accurate notes from lectures?

_____ 36. Do I use abbreviations for note taking?

_____ 37. Do I turn my notes into study sheets?

_____ 38. Do I consistently review my notes over a period of time?

MEMORY FOR BETTER GRADES

_____ 39. Do I understand how the three types of memory work for me?

_____ 40. Do I use a variety of techniques to memorize besides reading information over and over?

_____ 41. Do I use efficient ways to study and review for tests?

_____ 42. When I take tests, do I remember enough information to get the grades I want?

TEST TAKING

_____ 43. Do I begin studying from the first day a new unit is introduced?

_____ 44. While taking a test, do I carefully follow directions?

_____ 45. Do I know strategies for taking different kinds of tests?

_____ 46. Do I keep old tests and notes to use for mid-terms and finals?

_____ 47. Do I analyze my errors on tests to determine a pattern?

_____ 48. Do I effectively prepare for mid-terms and final exams?

_____ 49. Am I pleased with my current grades?

HANDLING HOMEWORK

_____ 50. Do I include all the directions of an assignment in my planner or cell phone?

_____ 51. Do I do homework in an environment that allows me to concentrate?

_____ 52. Do I exert enough thought and effort to learn something meaningful from my assignments?

_____ 53. Do I complete and turn in my homework by its due date?

STRESS MANAGEMENT

_____ 54. Am I confident that I can do well in school?

_____ 55. Do I usually feel calm and relaxed about school?

_____ 56. Do I know and use strategies to help me reduce stress?

WHAT IS YOUR STUDY SKILLS RATING?   SCORE: _____

50-56 Correct is 90% – 100% Superior

45-49 Correct is 80% – 89% Good

40-44 Correct is 70% – 79% Average

Less than 40 Correct is below 70% – Needs Improvement

INTERPRETATION OF YOUR STUDY SKILLS ANSWERS:

Review each of your responses to analyze your specific study skills strengths and weaknesses. As you learn and apply the strategies in _Study Strategies Plus_, you'll begin to see that you can work smarter, more efficiently, and be the better student you really want to be.

⊃ **Now ask yourself:** How would my life be better if I could improve my skills?

(*Example: My parents would stop nagging me; I would get better grades.*)

1.	
2.	
3.	
4.	

⊃ **Personal Goals:** Now that you have evaluated your present executive functioning and study skills, what are your personal goals?

1.	
2.	
3.	
4.	

Now that you've thought about how your life could be better if you develop new and more efficient study skills, read Jaime's story about how her life improved after she started using the strategies from *Study Strategies Plus*.

Jaime's Story

School has been a struggle for me since I can remember. It was never because I was lazy or gave up or didn't have a support system. In fact, it was exactly the opposite. I worked hard and I worked consistently, and at times my parents worked just as hard as I did to help me. I should have been excelling as a student, but I wasn't. Teachers and tutors were mystified since according to them I was "doing everything right."

After many disappointing report cards and lots of tears, I gradually lost faith in my ability to succeed academically. Like most teens, I let my failures in school negatively affect every aspect of my life, but that was the past. I'm now proud to say that as an honor roll student graduating high school, I no longer see myself in a negative light because of academic failures. I can literally pinpoint why: Study Strategies Plus. I'm not being melodramatic when I say that Study Strategies Plus changed my life. At first I was hesitant to learn new methods because I feared failure. My mistake. I learned how to take notes, how to memorize, and how to study. I learned how to succeed in school, even if it was not through the traditional note card and "cramming" method my classmates use. It's definitely hard work, but the satisfaction and joy I get from receiving good grades is worth every second.

— Jaime O'Connor

Jaime's story can be your story, too!

Chapter Two

EXECUTIVE FUNCTIONING

> "If the human brain were so simple
> that we could understand it,
> we would be so simple that we couldn't."
>
> —Emerson M. Pugh

Jen was popular with her schoolmates, and she decided to throw a party at her house to celebrate the end of the school year. She was super excited and told her parents and closest friends that she was going to have a party but said little more as she wanted to do it all herself.

Jen sat at her desk night after night trying to plan the party. She made lists of friends to invite, the food she wanted to serve, and music to play. Each night as she began her planning, either her phone would ring or she would be distracted by the television, her dog wanting attention, or other things going on around her. Although she liked the idea of planning the party, she never quite got around to doing so.

About a week before the date of her party, Jen hadn't even sent out invitations and now she didn't have time to buy any or mail them. She decided to text and email her friends instead to let them know the date and time of the party, but she didn't know some of her friend's email addresses and kept forgetting to ask them. She did, however, get in touch with several of her friends and invited them.

Unfortunately, she didn't mention the party to her parents until the day before it was to happen. Her parent(s) told her that they were having a party of their own that night, and she would have to do hers on another date. Jen contacted her friends again to tell them the party would be postponed until the next day (Sunday).

In the meantime, word had spread around the school about Jen's Saturday night party and some people showed up only to be greeted by her parents, their friends, and worst of all, THEIR MUSIC!

By Sunday, Jen had forgotten to buy the food or organize her music. Unfortunately, many of the people she did tell about the change of plans couldn't make it. Only four of Jen's friends showed up on Sunday. They ate leftover food from her parent's party, played some random music, and tried their best to support a disappointed Jen.

What were some of Jen's mistakes?

■ She didn't take the time to write a plan or ask herself the right questions about what steps needed to be taken to accomplish her goals.

■ She had good intentions, but poor follow through because she often got distracted.

■ She didn't prioritize what was important to do and left things for the last minute.

■ Though she knew what she needed, she didn't organize her time or actions to get the invitations sent out on time, pick the food she was going to serve, and select the music.

■ Most importantly, she forgot to tell her parents about the party and before she set a new date she didn't check with her friends to see if they could come then.

Luckily, Jen threw another party at the end of the summer. This time she got her mother and friends to help her organize it. Jen learned a valuable experience from all of this, namely, that she has to plan more carefully to make a successful party.

What are Executive Functions?

Executive functions are a group of skills that help us manage the way we think and act. To succeed in our complex world, we need to use executive functions to solve problems. The human brain is divided into different regions that control different aspects of our bodily functions, our senses, our thinking processes, and our behavior. One of these brain regions, the prefrontal cortex, the most modern part of our brain, is believed to be the area that is responsible for managing executive functions. There are connections from this area to other parts of our brain.

Executive functions give you the ability to control emotions and behavior, plan actions, manage time, retain and use information stored memory, focus attention, organize, monitor behavior, and to motivate to start and complete tasks. As you can imagine, executive functions are extremely important to you, especially when you are learning and problem solving in school. They also help you manage your behavior when you are with your friends, so you don't say or do things that would be inappropriate. With good executive functioning skills you can choose the appropriate behavior for the right setting, plan your actions, and imagine how things will turn out before you act so you can create a new plan if you need to.

To understand executive functioning, let's think about situations in your everyday life:

EF SKILLS INVOLVING THINKING	POSITIVE EXAMPLES OF BEHAVIOR
Organization	You organize your work space and arrange your school supplies in designated, easy to find places.
Time Management	You can estimate how long a task will take and then pace yourself so you finish on time.
Initiation and Task Completion	You have a plan to study at a certain time, and even though your friends invite you to join them for a fun outing, you are able to tell them no. You start studying and work until you are finished.
Planning and Prioritizing	Despite feeling overwhelmed with homework, tests and after-school activities, you are able to set up a plan and decide the order of what to do so it all gets done.
Self-monitoring and Metacognition	You identify the reasons for a disappointing test grade and how to do better on the next test.
Working Memory	The science teacher verbally assigns a project, but before you can write it into your agenda, your buddy asks you a question about a math problem. After you answer him, you are able to go back and correctly write the science assignment in your planner.

The following skills are also essential for efficient executive functioning. However, for the purpose of guiding you to attain effective study skills, we refer to them only when they are relevant to the study strategies that we introduce.

EF SKILLS INVOLVING DOING (BEHAVIOR)	POSITIVE EXAMPLES OF BEHAVIOR
Response inhibition	You do not react to the taunts of a bully; doing homework instead of going out with friends
Shifting (flexibility)	You change the topic of the report after finding that there isn't enough useful information
Emotional control	You know a test is super-important, yet you are able to relax enough to do your best

Not everyone has the same ability to use their executive function skills. Some people are better planners than others, some people have a better sense of time and organization, some remember information easier and for longer amounts of time, and some people have good self-control over their behavior while others have trouble controlling their behavior or emotions. Some people think about their behavior and plan their actions carefully while others are more quick to react. These individual differences in people make us more interesting.

Executive functioning skills develop as we mature. This is also a good thing because life becomes more complicated as we get older (i.e., more teachers, more homework, more activities to keep track of, more difficult problems to solve, etc.). We need more mature executive function skills to handle this complexity. However, even with maturation, some people have difficulty in some areas of executive functioning so they need to practice these skills to make them stronger.

The several chapters in *Study Strategies Plus* focus on executive function skills that are very important for school success. In each chapter, we will explain what the executive function skill is, why it is important, and strategies and practice activities that you can do to strengthen the skill if you believe you have trouble in that area. The executive function skills we will cover are:

- Organization
- Time Management
- Task Initiation and Completion (starting and finishing)
- Planning and Prioritizing
- Self-Monitoring and Metacognition

Chapter Three

ORGANIZATION

> "I find it helps to organize chores into categories:
> Things I won't do now;
> Things I won't do later; Things I'll never do."
>
> —cartoon character, Maxine

These are the skills that will be covered in this chapter.

> Organizing your surroundings
>
> Creating a system to organize
>
> Keeping track of grades
>
> Using an assignment planner

Amy's room is filled with heaps of "stuff." She throws that stuff wherever it happens to land. That means Amy has to spend lots of time hunting for school papers, pencils, and pens. ("Where is that study guide for tomorrow's unit test?") Her mornings are chaotic as she again begins her hunt. This time she's searching for clean clothes and the homework she truly did last night. Sometimes even if Amy remembered to finish her homework, she doesn't always take it to school and turn it in. Amy is frustrated but unclear about how to become better organized.

What is Organization?

Organization is a very important executive function. It is the ability to keep track of information, time, and materials. As we get older, our lives become more complicated, and we need to develop systems that will help us stay organized. Elementary school students, for instance, don't have many decisions to make on their own and their time is managed by parents and teachers. As we go through school, we make more of our own decisions and juggle more tasks so we must become proficient at self-management.

Some people are "born" organizers. They find it easy to be organized, and they just do it naturally. They prefer to keep their rooms neat, and they keep their belongings organized with little effort. Organization is as natural to them as breathing. For others, getting organized and staying organized requires a huge effort. Often students who have trouble organizing are labeled as lazy or procrastinators, but they just may not have good organization skills. If you have trouble with organization, we hope to teach you some of these skills in this chapter and others.

Can a person learn organization and how to maintain it? There are many books written to teach people how to be organized so we think it is a skill you can learn with practice. To be an effective organizer you have to THINK about organization. You can't just let piles get higher and clutter gather around you. You have to be aware of your surroundings. Organization is not a "one-and-done" activity. It is something you need to do regularly.

Practice Activity: Decide for Yourself! Do I Need to be Better Organized?

Take an honest look at yourself and your surroundings. Do you need to be better organized? Is disorganization affecting your performance in school or your relationships with family and friends? If the answer to either of these questions is YES, then take a look at areas where your organization could be improved.

Directions:

1. Check off from the list below the areas in which you think you could be better organized.

   ☐ Bedroom   ☐ Bathroom   ☐ Closet

   ☐ Desk and dresser drawers   ☐ Desk top   ☐ Bookbag or notebooks for school

   ☐ Car   ☐ Locker at school

   ☐ Other places _____

2. Make a plan to organize two or three of the areas you selected above and choose a day to carry out the plan. See the sample plan below.

   Sample plan:

   My room is a mess. I can't find things easily. On Saturday I am going to go through my closet, throw out all the stuff I don't need, and organize the stuff I want to keep. Then I'm going to celebrate with my friend.

   Write two or three other plans below that you would like to follow.

   _____

   _____

   _____

   _____

   _____

   _____

Practice Activity: Organize Your Study Area and Materials

1. Materials you'll need:
   a. one or more large garbage bags
   b. letter-size file box with hanging files, file folders, and labels

2. Cleaning up your room:

   a. Glance around your room and throw out anything that doesn't belong there. (Hint: used pizza cartons don't belong under your bed).

   b. Look again and this time, pick up papers. Divide them into two piles: **Keep** and **Throw Out**. Be decisive and DO NOT have a "maybe" pile. Immediately discard the "throw out" pile.

   c. Divide the "Keep" papers into categories and make files according to class.

   d. Label a file folder for each, such as "math: notes" or "math: past tests."

   e. Place file folders into the hanging file box or any good sized box or carton.

   f. List any materials and supplies you need. (Ask yourself: How will I use these supplies?)

   g. Decide where you will keep these supplies. (Ask yourself: If I place this here, will I see it? Will it be easily accessible?)

⊃ **Tip:** After your room is arranged in the way that's best for you, take a picture of it so in a few months, when it may be disorganized again (though we hope not), you can recall just where you wanted everything.

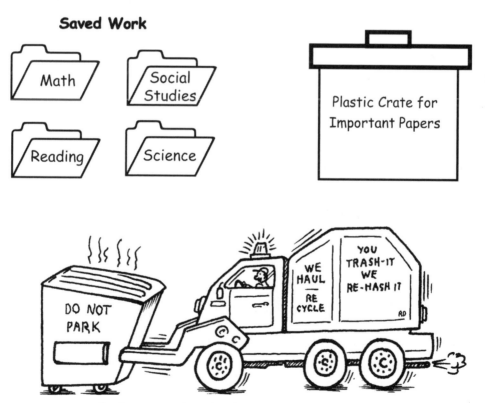

Garbage truck to haul away unimportant papers!

Practice Activity: Organize Your Bookbag

An organized bookbag can be key to better grades. Assignments, important papers, notes, and books can mysteriously disappear in a messy bag. Read Bookbag Boggle below.

Directions: Look at the contents of your bookbag and answer these questions by circling "Y" for Yes or "N" for No.

Bookbag Boggle

		Question:	If your answer is Yes:
Y	N	1. Is anything moving?	*Call the local humane society.*
Y	N	2. Are there papers you've been looking for that have been missing for months?	*File them in a labeled folder so you can find them before you graduate.*
Y	N	3. Are there papers you no longer need to carry to and from school?	*If they're old tests or important notes, take them home and file them. If you don't need them again, trash them now!*
Y	N	4. Are there books or folders without labels so you can't tell whether they're for science or English?	*Get a different color folder for each class. If you use a 3-ring binder, get dividers and label them.*
Y	N	5. Are notes from various classes thrown in one heap?	*Divide, label, and file them.*
Y	N	6. Do you feel liberated from your mess and much better organized?	*You have the power to keep this great feeling going by taking five minutes once a week to clean out your bookbag, organize folders and papers, and throw out whatever you don't need. You'll be so much happier if you do!*

Strategy: Organize Your Grades

Keeping your materials and study area organized allows you to be in control of your environment. Tracking your grades allows you to be in control of your learning. If you use the following strategy, you will keep track of your grades on a weekly basis to monitor how you are doing. That will allow you to make any changes you need to get the grades you want.

Practice Activity: Organize Your Grades

Directions: Refer to the sample grade chart following these instructions.

1. Write your name, circle the number of the current grading quarter and write its beginning date.

2. In the left "Course/Grade" column, write each of your courses and the grades you want to achieve.

3. Write in all the grades you receive during each week. Use the grade key on the chart so you know what this grade is for.

4. Review weekly to make sure you are meeting your goals.

GRADE CHART

Quarter 1 ②3 4
Beginning Date _Nov 11_

Name: _Chris_

KEY:
T = Test   Q = Quiz
HW = Homework   P = Project

COURSE	Week 1	Week 2	Week 3	Week 4	Week 5	Week 6	Week 7	Week 8	Week 9	Report Card Grade
English Grade I want __A__	Q 98 T 90	HW A T 100	P 102							
Bio Grade I want __B__	Lab 89 HW 92	T 72	Q 82							
Algebra Grade I want __B__	HW 92 Q 98	HW 98 T 77 P 90	HW 92 T 89							
World History Grade I want __A__	T 90 HW 100	Q 88 HW 98	T 90							

GRADE CHART

Quarter 1 2 3 4

Beginning Date _____

Name: _____

KEY:
T = Test   Q = Quiz
HW = Homework   P = Project

COURSE	Week 1	Week 2	Week 3	Week 4	Week 5	Week 6	Week 7	Week 8	Week 9	Report Card Grade
Grade I want___										
Grade I want___										
Grade I want___										
Grade I want___										
Grade I want___										
Grade I want___										
Grade I want___										

Strategy: Tips to Help You Work More Efficiently

What you can do:	Why you would do it:	How you can do it:
Find a place to study that is free of distractions.	You want to pay undivided attention to work.	Make and label three piles of what is on your desk, shelves and in drawers: "file, trash, need in sight."
Use a desk or flat surface that is large enough to spread out work.	Clutter-free areas allow clutter-free thinking.	Use a desk, a plank of wood, or a large table designated for homework.
Buy or make containers for school supplies such as pens, papers, scissors, file folders, etc. and shelves or any areas that are at eye level and open.	Easy access allows less procrastination and wasted time searching for materials. Some people need to see their items while others need to have them within reach.	Use cans, tins, plastic containers or store-bought containers.
Devise a system for filing and keeping papers and supplies.	Logical systems promote organization and use.	Buy an accordion-style file folder and label per class; a 4X6 or 5X7 file box with dividers for vocabulary or other flash cards; a crate with one hanging folder per class and one pocket folder in each per grading period (all labeled)
Buy (or make) a calendar with large, blank boxes.	Long-term (monthly) planning allows you to see a larger picture of the upcoming activities.	Fill in family and after-school activities, tests, projects, etc. in each day's box. Hang it where it is clearly visible.
Buy a planner if the school doesn't supply one.	It encourages logging details of daily and weekly assignments, which makes homework and tests more manageable.	Decide which format is best for your needs.

Strategy: Practice Good Organizing Habits

Our space can become messy quite easily. When we are busy it is not always easy to take the time to put things away and stay organized. Sometimes we just want to "chill" and not worry about straightening up. This is fine once in awhile, but if we practice using good organizing behaviors, they will eventually become habits.

Below are descriptions of four helpful organizing habits (using routines, making checklists, finding a place for things you often misplace, and decluttering):

1. Decide on a routine and follow it.

   Sticking to a routine helps you automate tasks. Routines take the decision-making out of the process. For example, you come home from school and have about an hour of homework to do. If you don't have a homework routine established, you might waste time thinking about when you should do homework, where you should do it, and how long you will work on it. If you have a homework routine established all these decisions have already been made for you. Below are some examples of other routines that are important to incorporate in your daily life.

   - Make your bed every day.
   - Put away your clean clothes and put dirty clothes in the laundry every day.
   - Walk the dog every morning before breakfast.
   - Throw the trash out in your room every day.
   - Clean out your bookbag every Sunday.
   - Make a To Do List every day.
   - Do your homework.
   - Put things back after you use them every day.
   - Never leave a room empty handed.
   - File, don't pile papers.

2. Make a checklist and cross things off.

   Checklists are a great way to help you organize your thoughts about what you need to do. Some people make "mental checklists" as they think about the things they need to do; others write their checklists on paper or send themselves digital reminders and lists. If you are new to organizing, we suggest you use written checklists because they can serve as prompts to get things done. Your checklist can become a "To Do List" that you use to keep track of your success throughout the day. Cross out tasks as you complete them.

3. Make a place for things and put them where they belong.

   If you have trouble remembering where you put things, then get into the habit of putting things in the same place all the time. For example, leave your keys, cell phone, iPod, etc. in the same place every single time you walk through the door of your apartment or house. If you need them you will know where they are.

4. Declutter regularly.

Make a decision to declutter. Choose a place to start and work on it everyday for at least five minutes. Five minutes won't make a big dent in a volcano of clutter that may have erupted in your room, your desk, your bathroom, or elsewhere, but it is a start. Celebrate your beginning. Take five minutes today, another five tomorrow, and so on. In a few days you will have made progress in cleaning your closet, rearranging your desk and throwing old stuff away, or tidying your room.

Try to make your area "clutter-proof" by not allowing items to build up anymore. Get into the routine of putting or throwing things away. If you feel motivated and energetic, schedule a decluttering evening or weekend. Make a list of the areas that need to be decluttered and go for it.

Practice Activity: Identify a New Routine That Will Help You Become Better Organized

Directions: Write one new routine you could start that will help you become better organized and keep track of your progress implementing the new routine for the next seven days.

Describe your new routine (what you will do and how often).

Start Date _____	Rate yourself 1 - 10 (poor to excellent)	Comments (what you did and how you could improve)
Day 1		
Day 2		
Day 3		
Day 4		
Day 5		
Day 6		
Day 7		

Practice Activity: Declutter Schedule

Directions: Select a shelf, a desktop, a closet, a room, your bookbag, etc. that you want to declutter.

Describe what you will declutter (what will you do and how often).

Start Date _____	How much time will I budget?	Rate yourself 1 - 10	Comments (describe what you did and how you could improve)
Day 1			
Day 2			
Day 3			
Day 4			
Day 5			
Day 6			
Day 7			

⊃ **Now ask yourself:**

How will my life be better if I were more organized?

1.	
2.	

Teachers: What can you do?

What you can do:	Why you would do it:
1. Explicitly teach specific strategies	To teach how to organize bookbags, lockers, desk, and files
2. Model and do think-alouds	To show how you organize your own materials and work
3. Display posters in the classroom	To remind students how to stay organized
4. Get feedback from your class about how these strategies are working	For students to brainstorm changes that might work better for them
5. Keep your supplies organized and visible, including: ■ a file box or accordion folder of files, each one labeled by class, and then by quarter or semester ■ a tackle-type supply box ■ binders or folders, depending upon your requirements ■ paper ■ large calendar and/or planner	To model examples of efficient organization
6. Require each student to keep a 3-ring binder, which could include: ■ tabbed dividers, preferably with pockets to be labeled "homework," "handouts" and "class notes," etc.	To encourage uniform organization
7. Periodically check binders to see if students are staying organized ■ Grade students' efforts (each quarters' total binder—check grade could equal one quiz grade) ■ Give open-note quizzes from information that can be found only in notes and handouts kept in the binder	To reinforce consistent maintenance of organization
8. Send parents an outline of your requirements (folders, supplies, etc.) and the organizational strategies you teach your class	To engage parents in your quest to encourage organization in your students

Other teaching tips:

1. Lead a class discussion about the benefits of keeping work spaces organized. The class will then brainstorm how to organize their rooms at home, keeping their personal learning styles in mind.

2. Assign the class to organize their personal workspaces and then take a picture or make a video of the before and after.

3. Encourage humor, creativity, specific suggestions, and reasons for how they organized their spaces.

Chapter Four

TIME MANAGEMENT

> **"If it weren't for the last minute,
> I wouldn't get anything done."**
>
> —Author Unknown

These are the skills that will be covered in this chapter.

Sensing time
Estimating time
Scheduling time

Josh never has enough time to hang out with friends or chill. He's always rushing from one activity to another, and although he thinks he leaves enough time, he's often late. He has six different teachers who give so much homework that every night he's up until midnight. Every time he thinks one assignment will take 20 minutes, it takes 60. He's turned in so many late assignments and asked for so many time extensions that teachers think the only food his dog eats is his homework!

What is Time Management?

Time management is another important executive function. Time management involves the ability to estimate how long something will take to complete and meet deadlines. Effectively managing time is crucial, and when we aren't good at it, it can undermine our ability to honor obligations or have enough time to accomplish what we want (including hanging out with friends and relaxing). It also can affect others' views of whether we are reliable.

Students with poor time management skills often have trouble starting and finishing tasks on time. They have difficulty estimating how long it takes to complete a task or a project, have trouble getting to appointments on time, and have challenges adhering to a schedule.

Why do some people have good time management and others do not? We don't really know the answer to that, but we do know that good time management requires a good "sense" of time or an awareness of time, self-monitoring to check the time, and the ability to adjust your behavior to avoid running out of time (e.g., being flexible with your priorities, speeding up when necessary, skipping something, delegating a job to someone else).

You have to THINK about time to be an effective time manager. You can't just let time pass and be unaware of it. You must make it a priority to do things on time. You have to budget your time and forecast how your activities will fit into the time slots that you allotted. Effective time managers must also meet deadlines. This requires having an idea of what you need to do, the skills and resources to do it, and maintaining focus on the task so you don't become distracted.

Strategy: Developing a Good Sense of Time

What do we mean by "sense of time?"

Human beings, animals, plants, and other living creatures all have internal, or biological, clocks. These clocks signal people to wake up, go to sleep, and eat; plants to bloom; bears to store food to prepare for hibernation during the winter; and birds to fly south for the winter to avoid cold weather. Internal clocks are essential for the survival of many species. They are "hard-wired" in the brain.

The ability to sense time is a very important executive function of the human brain, not only for purposes of survival, but for managing our lives efficiently. For some people, their internal clock seems to tick loudly in their mind, and they are very aware of time. For others, their internal clock is more in the background. If your internal clock clicks too quietly, it may not give you the signals you need to perform tasks in a punctual manner.

If you want to improve your sense of time try the following strategies:

1. Wear a watch and put more clocks around your house so you can check the time more frequently.

2. Make a habit of checking the time regularly throughout the day. If you don't know what time it is, you won't be able to manage it very well.

3. Wear a watch that beeps or vibrates (they sell different brands online) or use apps on your mobile device to remind you when it is time to do something.

4. During the day, ask yourself questions like— "Am I on time?" or "What should I be doing at this time?" These types of questions (which we call metacognitive questions) will keep time at the forefront of your mind rather than in the background.

5. To keep yourself focused on tasks and do things on time, it sometimes helps to use a countdown timer (a cooking timer, a stopwatch on your mobile device) that you set to alert you when you should have a task finished. Try to "beat the timer" and finish before the alarm goes off to see if you estimated time correctly.

6. Of course, using a planner will help. You can use the Weekly Schedule that is discussed in this book or you can make a daily schedule. Using a daily or weekly schedule forces you to think about how you will spend your time and may improve your overall sense of time. To Do Lists can also be helpful in this regard. It is important to check your schedule or To Do List frequently so you can make sure you are using the time you set aside properly.

Practice Activity: Sensing Time

This activity will help you improve sense of time. For example, do you have a good idea of how long it takes you to get out of bed after you are awakened, brush your teeth, and get dressed and eat breakfast? In the table below, time the regular activities you do so you are familiar with how long they take. We've given you one example.

Date	What did you do?	How long did it take?
3/5	took a shower	10 minutes

Strategy: Estimating Time

Some people are great at judging how much time it will take to get something done. Others either overestimate or underestimate the amount of time a task will require. Overestimators complete tasks quicker than they expected. They generally have extra time and can shift their attention to other things.

Underestimators don't leave enough time to finish a task and often run out of time. This can easily happen when you are not familiar with the work. For example, you may have thought a task is simpler than it actually is, or you may not have anticipated certain events to occur that can be distracting and cause delays. If this happens too much you could have piles of school work that you don't have time to complete and your grades could suffer.

Accurate time estimation is important in all kinds of tasks: school work, projects around the home, planning vacations, and in activities with friends. Sometimes it just takes a few minutes to think about a project or a task before you jump to an inaccurate conclusion about how long it will take to complete. Use the next practice activity to improve your time estimation skills.

Practice Activity: Estimating Time Accurately

Step 1: Understand what is required to complete the task.

Step 2: List the things you will need to do to complete the task.

Step 3: Decide who you will need to involve.

Step 4: Determine what materials you will need.

Step 5: Make your estimate.

Directions: Your history teacher has given you a homework assignment to read a 25 page chapter in your book and to write 10 multiple choice questions about the information you learned. Once you have written the questions, you are to give your test to another student in the class to evaluate their knowledge. Write the information needed for each of the steps below.

1. Write what is required to complete the task.

_____

_____

2. Write the order in which you will need to do things to complete the task.

_____

_____

3. Decide who you will need to involve.

_____

_____

4. Determine what materials you will need.

_____

_____

5. How much time will this take?

_____

_____

Strategy: Use a Planner to Write Down Assignments and to Organize Your Time

Many students use planners to remind them of upcoming appointments, to write down their assignments or set time aside for homework and studying. Smart phones, iPads®, and other mobile devices have easy-to-use calendar applications that can track this information.

For example, planners are great for making a study schedule to prepare for tests. Cramming the night before a test isn't the most effective way to study. You will learn better by studying in smaller chunks each day, starting a few days before a test by reviewing your notes, re-reading your text book, going over old tests, etc. Planning the times that you will set aside for this is helpful.

We have included an example of a Weekly Schedule Sheet. Review the sheet that follows to see a sample of how to plan your week. This student used her Weekly Schedule Sheet to allot time for homework each day, review time for studying notes and making a study guide, and appointments for the dentist, club meetings, etc.

Practice Activity: How to use a weekly schedule sheet to budget your time.

In the time estimation activity, you saw how long it took to complete your daily activities. You are now ready to use that awareness to evaluate how long you have available versus how long you actually take for homework and studying. You will then be able to budget your time more realistically and efficiently.

Directions: Fill out your weekly schedule (Refer to the illustration of the sample schedule):

1. Write your after-school activities, such as practices, work, family events, etc. in the time spaces for each day. This shows you the times you **don't have free** to do homework or study.

2. Draw a box around the remaining empty spaces which show the time you have available to do homework and study.

3. For each day, add the number of hours you have available and write them in the "Available Time" spaces at the bottom of the schedule.

4. Look at the schedule sheet to get a clear picture of what your week will look like.

5. As you do your homework or study each day, in the appropriate time slot, write the subject and how long it takes you. For example, if on Monday you do science homework from 5:00 to 5:30 PM, you will write it in Monday's time slot. Refer to the weekly schedule sample.

6. Add the time you needed for each day's school work and enter that number in the space marked "Time Used For Study" at the bottom of the schedule sheet.

7. Did you have enough time to get everything done for schoolwork and study? ____yes ____no

8. If not, use the blank schedule to make changes.

At the end of the week, review how your changes helped you to budget your time. Use this information to budget your study time from now on.

Copy the blank schedule sheet if you would like to use it for more than one week.

WEEKLY SCHEDULE SHEET

WEEK OF <u>3/2</u>

TIME	Monday	Tuesday	Wednesday	Thursday	Friday	Saturday	Sunday
4:00 - 5:00 or earlier	volleyball practice	club meeting	volleyball practice	dentist	bring home math sheets for review	volleyball game	
5:00 - 5:30	review Spanish verbs for quiz						read English p.110-120
5:30 - 6:00	dinner			email team about Sat.			and annotate
6:00 - 6:30		dinner	dinner	dinner			Watch Spanish cable show
6:30 - 7:00	math: p.121 #3-11	math: p.123 #4-23	review science notes				
7:00 - 7:30	read history (150-175)+	read science notes	make science study guide	review history notes from week			review math study guide
7:30 - 8:00	take notes	read science hand-out-test Thursday	break	review Spanish verbs			
8:00 - 8:30	break	relax	read English p.95-110	prepare for math review class	movies		organize next week's work
8:30 - 9:00	call Sam to get notes		+annotate	tomorrow			
9:00 - 9:30	TV, relax		bed				
9:30 - 10:00							
10:00 - 10:30 or after							
AVAILABLE TIME / TIME USED FOR STUDY	3 hrs. / 2.5 hrs.	1.5 hrs. / 1.5 hrs.	2 hrs. / 2 hrs.	2 hrs. / 2 hrs.	0 / 0	0 / 0	3 hrs. / 2.5 hrs.

⟳ Now ask yourself:

How will my life be better now that I can manage my time more efficiently?

1.	
2.	

WEEKLY SCHEDULE SHEET

WEEK OF _____

TIME	Monday	Tuesday	Wednesday	Thursday	Friday	Saturday	Sunday
4:00 - 5:00 or earlier							
5:00 - 5:30							
5:30 - 6:00							
6:00 - 6:30							
6:30 - 7:00							
7:00 - 7:30							
7:30 - 8:00							
8:00 - 8:30							
8:30 - 9:00							
9:00 - 9:30							
9:30 - 10:00							
10:00 - 10:30 or after							
AVAILABLE TIME / TIME USED FOR STUDY							

This form may be reproduced for personal use.

Chapter Five

STARTING, FOCUSING, AND FINISHING

> "It's not that I'm so smart;
> it's just that I stay with problems longer."
> —Albert Einstein

These are the skills that will be covered in this chapter.

Starting assignments without procrastinating
Staying focused on assignments until they are completed
Finishing assignments on time

Alex has problems getting started on his work. Two weeks ago he was given an assignment to read a book about the sinking of the Titanic and then write a review of it. He wasn't very interested in the book assigned to him, and he hated to write. Each night (even though he had promised himself to start the project) he found other things to do. A few nights he managed to get started, but he lost interest and turned his attention to other things that were more fun. He realized that he couldn't procrastinate any longer because the assignment was due tomorrow. He had also promised his mother that he would watch his younger brother that night, and he couldn't possibly do both.

Does this sound familiar? You could be a procrastinator who delays what is boring or tedious. Then when you realize you haven't done what you need to do, you feel pressured, nervous, and upset.

This section is for you (actually for all of us who share your procrastinator's pain). Here are some ideas to help you begin and complete tasks even when you'd rather be doing anything else.

What is Self-activation and Focus?

Self-activation (the word for getting yourself started) is the executive function that turns your engine on and keeps you going. Some cars go from 0 to 60 miles per hour in 10 seconds and some can do it in four. Similarly, people also accelerate at different rates. Some are quick to start a task and are able to stay with it and complete it and others are slower to start and "run out of gas" before they finish. Some procrastinate so often that they rarely start anything when they should.

Both external and internal pressure can affect when and how we do things. External pressure comes from outside of ourselves, usually from other people (e.g., parents, teachers, bosses) or institutions (e.g., school). People are more likely to start and complete tasks when high external pressure is exerted on them and they face a negative consequence (e.g., get the book report in tomorrow or you will fail) or a positive one (e.g., if you get the book report in by tomorrow you will get extra credit). Internal pressure is motivation or drive that comes from within ourselves that causes us to act. Many different factors can affect internal motivation (e.g., our personal goals and values, behavior we learned from others, self-confidence, whether or not we enjoy the activity, etc.).

Task initiation is not simple. It requires good executive functioning plus external or internal pressure that can increase our motivation and drive. Success in school and in life depends on our ability to start and complete tasks, regardless of whether they are enjoyable or interesting.

Obviously after starting a task you have to stay focused to complete it. To focus is to concentrate on a specific central point or idea. Focusing for a significant amount of time requires attention and the ability to eliminate distractions. For simple, routine tasks (e.g., getting dressed, brushing your teeth, walking to your friend's house) only small amounts of focus are usually required since we are used to doing these things. New or more complex tasks (e.g., studying for an exam, writing an essay about Napoleon Bonaparte, planning a date with your friends) require more intense and sustained focus. Focus enables us to concentrate on a task long enough and hard enough to get it accomplished efficiently and correctly.

Everyone has the ability to focus, but some people are better at it than others. Scientists think that the ability to focus starts in the brain, but it can be affected by all sorts of things such as your motivation to complete a task, your interest in the task, whether you are hungry or tired, or your environment. Like time management, organization, and planning, focus is an executive function that can be trained. You can improve your focus through practice and by THINKING about staying focused. You shouldn't take focus for granted and think of it as some "automatic" behavior that you can't control. Although some people have a hard time focusing, practice can help improve this skill. Staying focused requires effort and like most things in life, you get out what you put in.

Strategy: Common Mistakes Procrastinators Make

Everyone procrastinates some of the time, but some students are chronic procrastinators. They avoid unpleasant or difficult tasks and intentionally look for other things to do that are more enjoyable. They don't get their school assignments done on time, are late for class, don't keep dates with their friends, miss opportunities to buy concert tickets, put off exercising, don't make decisions on time, or buy holiday gifts at the last minute.

Procrastinators commonly make the following mistakes:

1. They think they can get things done quicker than they actually can.

2. They think they have more time to get something done than they actually have.

3. They think they have to be in the right mood to do something.

4. They look for distractions to avoid starting unpleasant tasks.

5. They seek immediate gratification rather than wait for it.

Practice Activity: Understanding Your Procrastination

Describe a task that you recently delayed completing.

_____

_____

_____

Explain why you procrastinated.

_____

_____

_____

Which of the common mistakes listed above might explain your procrastination?

_____

_____

_____

Did you eventually complete the task? What got you started?

_____

_____

_____

Strategy: Overcoming Procrastination

Chronic procrastinators feel bad about their behavior. They would like to change, but they find it difficult to do so. Psychologists agree that procrastination is difficult to overcome. Below are some tips that might help you manage procrastination if you find this is a problem in your life.

Be Honest with Yourself and Others

1. Recognize when you are procrastinating, and be honest with yourself about your procrastination.

2. Think of procrastination as a habit. The more you do it, the stronger it becomes.

3. Face procrastination head on! Challenge yourself and resist the desire to avoid or delay doing things that are unpleasant, tedious, or require effort.

4. Admit to others (e.g., parents, teachers, friends) that you need help with procrastination and ask for their assistance.

Stay Fit and Healthy

5. Make sure you get enough rest and eat healthy so your body is strong and your brain is alert.

6. Exercise to stay energized.

Manage Your Feelings

7. Worry about success or lack of self-confidence can cause us to avoid or delay starting a task. Try to think positively to reduce stress and worry.

8. Create happy times. Balance out a tough day with some pleasant experiences. These positive experiences can energize you to do more.

9. Be patient with yourself and recognize that it takes time to overcome procrastination.

Change Your Thoughts and Behavior

10. Create an affirmation statement (e.g., "Do it now.") and silently recite it throughout the day.

11. Don't wait for the "right" time or the "right" mood to get started on a task.

12. Do important tasks BEFORE you fill your time with unimportant busy work (e.g., checking email, texting a friend, going online, etc).

13. Don't look for distractions. They prolong procrastination.

14. Make a simple "To Do List" and stick to it. Reward yourself when you complete a task.

15. Identify when you work best (e.g., morning, after school, at night)

Practice Activity

Directions: Consider the 15 points listed above and write the ones that you think will work best for you to overcome procrastination.

_____

_____

_____

_____

_____

_____

_____

_____

_____

_____

Strategy: Reaching Your Goals in Time

The tips below will help you get started on tasks, remain focused, and help you finish tasks on time.

BEFORE YOU BEGIN:

1. Put your assignment into your planner or mobile device. Be sure to include:
   - details (due date, page numbers and directions)
   - date and time you will begin the assignment

2. Estimate how long it will take you to complete the task.

3. Choose triggers that will remind and encourage you to start the task:
   - set an alarm
   - ask someone to remind you to begin working

WHILE YOU ARE WORKING:

1. Pay attention to the trigger and begin the assignment.

2. Chunk your assignment by breaking it into smaller, more easily handled parts (like breaking a big chocolate bar into more manageable smaller chunks).

3. Time how long it takes you to complete the assignment.

4. Work for 20 minutes.

5. Take a 5-minute break. Set your alarm for 5 minutes and when it goes off, immediately get back to work. Estimate how long it will take you to do the task.

⟳ **You can reach your goal if you work until the task is completed.**

AFTER YOU ARE DONE:

1. Ask yourself if you are satisfied with your completed work. If not, go back and make revisions.

2. Compare your time estimation to the actual time it took you to complete the assignment (don't count break time!).

3. File your completed work in your homework folder, and then put it the folder into your book bag.

4. Take the book bag to school and turn in your work.

Practice Activity: Check Your Focus Habits

Directions: Read each of the following tips about focusing and put a check in the box indicating how often you use them to help you focus. When you have finished, think about the tips on the list that you might be able to incorporate in your routine to help you focus better.

Never	Sometimes	Usually	Rarely	
☐	☐	☐	☐	1. I close the door to the room where I am concentrating.
☐	☐	☐	☐	2. I break down tasks into small chunks.
☐	☐	☐	☐	3. I set a goal as to how much work I will complete or how much time I will spend.
☐	☐	☐	☐	4. I set a timer and focus on one thing until the time period ends.
☐	☐	☐	☐	5. I eat something to give my brain fuel to focus.
☐	☐	☐	☐	6. I turn off the computer, cell phone, television and other distractions.
☐	☐	☐	☐	7. I remind family or friends not to bother me.
☐	☐	☐	☐	8. I find a place where I can focus the best (e.g., favorite room, chair, etc.).
☐	☐	☐	☐	9. I keep something in my hands to play with (e.g., clay, a pen, a paper clip) because sometimes movement can help me focus.
☐	☐	☐	☐	10. I move about the room as I read/study/memorize because movement helps me focus.
☐	☐	☐	☐	11. Before starting a task, I review in my mind what I have to do to clarify my goals and objectives.
☐	☐	☐	☐	12. I take short breaks when I need them and do something to rest my mind.
☐	☐	☐	☐	13. I reward myself for staying on task and completing things.
☐	☐	☐	☐	14. I have a sign in my room that says "Stay Focused" or something to that effect.
☐	☐	☐	☐	15. I remind myself to do one thing at a time and ignore distractions.
☐	☐	☐	☐	16. When I feel overwhelmed by things I have to do, I take a deep breath, relax, and let go of fear and worry.
☐	☐	☐	☐	17. I tell myself, "It will only take two minutes" as a way to avoid procrastinations.
☐	☐	☐	☐	18. I write things down so I don't forget.
☐	☐	☐	☐	19. Before I start a task I meditate for a few minutes to empty my mind of distractions.
☐	☐	☐	☐	20. I organize my workspace and remove clutter so I won't be distracted.

Strategy: Tips on How to Stay Focused

1. Set a goal and envision the outcome. Goals should be specific, measurable, and attainable. Being able to envision a specific goal and reminding yourself of why you want to achieve it will help you stay focused.

2. Create enthusiasm about reaching your goal. Enthusiasm is to focus like gas is to a car. It gives your brain fuel to concentrate. When we are excited about something it is easier to stay focused. Plan a reward for yourself for staying focused and working toward completing your goal.

3. Plan and write down the steps you will take to reach your goal. This will give you clear focus of what you need to do.

4. Do one thing at a time. The biggest enemy of focus is distraction. As you work toward your goal, remind yourself to complete one thing before moving on to something else. It is easy to get "off task" so you must focus your efforts on one thing at a time.

5. Eliminate distractions and find a place where you focus the best. Consider the things that cause you to become distracted (television, video games, food, talking with a friend on the phone, texting, etc.). No matter how tempting these distractions might be, make up your mind to ignore them until you finish your work. You could use some of these distracters as a reward for staying focused. If you get distracted, remind yourself of the goal you want to accomplish and how you will feel once you do so.

6. Take breaks when needed. Pausing can give your brain the rest it needs to stay focused longer. Sometimes you need to tune-out to tune-in.

7. Ask family and friends for help. You may have to ask your family or friends for some privacy so that you can spend quality time on a project without them distracting you. They can also provide gentle reminders for you to stay on task.

Practice Activity: Plan to Stay Focused

Identify a specific task or project that you have to complete for school and answer the questions below.

1. Describe your goal for the project (be specific and realistic).

2. What is motivating you to stay focused and accomplish the goal?

3. List the steps you will take to accomplish the goal.

4. List the things that might affect your focus and describe how you will handle distractions.

5. What will you do to give your brain a break?

6. How will your family or friends help you achieve this goal?

Practice Activity: Staying Tuned In to Being Tuned In

As we explained earlier, staying focused when completing simple tasks (e.g., eating lunch, taking a walk, etc.) requires little effort and concentration. The more complicated a task is, the more focus it requires. Take a few minutes to evaluate how focused you generally are while completing the tasks listed below. In the space before each activity mark the following:

V – Very often have difficulty staying focused

O – Often have difficulty staying focused

S – Sometimes have difficulty staying focused, but not very much.

R – Rarely have difficulty staying focused

_____ 1. Listening in class.

_____ 2. Doing homework.

_____ 3. Reading a textbook.

_____ 4. Reading directions or instructions.

_____ 5. Studying for a test.

_____ 6. Watching television.

_____ 7. Conversing with a friend.

_____ 8. Driving a car.

_____ 9. Straightening up my room.

_____ 10. Playing a video game.

_____ 11. Eating.

_____ 12. Exercising.

Strategy: More Tips to Improve Your Focus

Activity	Tips
Listening in class	1. Sit near the teacher. 2. Don't let your mind wander. 3. Don't talk to others. 4. Before class, think about what the class is going to be about. 5. Take notes. 6. Ask questions. 7. Think about what the teacher is saying.
Doing homework **Reading a textbook** **Studying for tests**	1. Get something to eat or drink if you need it. 2. Tell your family you are going to do homework and you need privacy. 3. Find a quiet place in your home where you concentrate the best. 4. Refer to your planner to see exactly what you need to do. 5. Determine the order in which you want to tackle assignments. 6. Make sure you have all your materials available (books, notebook, paper, pens and pencils, computer, etc.). 7. Start your homework and take breaks when you need them. 8. Study for tests over a few days so you don't have to cram the night before an exam.
Straightening up your room	1. Consider how much you want to do (i.e., clean up entire room, work on a closet, clear your desk, sort your book bag). 2. Think about how you want to start and write down some of the steps that could become your checklist. 3. Go through each step on the checklist and cross out the things you complete. 4. When finished, make a plan to go on to the next thing you want to organize.
Driving your car	1. Make a rule: no calling, texting, checking email, or use of mobile devices for any reason while you are on the road. 2. Make sure you know how to get to the place you are going to so you don't get confused or distracted. 3. Keep your eyes on the road and your attention on traffic. Consider turning off the radio, etc. if you find it can be a distraction. 4. If you tend to be distractible while driving, remind yourself to pay attention to the road and other cars. Think about staying focused.

Strategy: Improve Time Management, Organization, and Planning

Other chapters in *Study Strategies Plus* provide strategies and activities to help you manage time, become better organized, and plan more effectively. Applying these strategies will also help you become better at task initiation and completion and reduce procrastination.

⊃ **Now ask yourself:**
How will my life be better now that I can start and finish my work in a timely fashion?

1.	
2.	

Teachers: What can you do?

Not every one who procrastinates is a procrastinator. Experts believe that about 20% of people who procrastinate are chronic procrastinators. They do it so often that they have very serious problems getting things done. Students may be unaware of the substantial problems that chronic procrastination can lead to and they may benefit from discussing this in class.

- Define what procrastination is.

- Discuss examples of procrastination and the effects it can have on student performance.

- Discuss the common mistakes that procrastinators make.

- Explain that most people who procrastinate would like to change because they are unhappy with their behavior.

- Discuss the steps that can be taken to overcome procrastination.

- Discuss with students what they do to help them stay focused.

- Point out the importance of time management, organization, and planning to help manage procrastination and improve task initiation and completion.

Chapter Six

PLANNING AND PRIORITIZING

> "If you don't know where you are going,
> you'll end up somewhere else."
>
> —Yogi Berra

These are the skills that will be covered in this chapter.

Evaluating how well you plan

Creating effective plans to accomplish goals

Following the steps in your plan

Setting priorities

Planning long term projects

Matt Lauer interviewed Michael Trapp, a pilot whose small plane crashed into Lake Huron. Lauer asked the pilot how he managed to survive in the water for 18 hours.

Trapp said his plane sputtered and crashed before he had time to secure a life preserver. As the plane descended into water, panic set in. Knowing that his only chance of survival depended solely upon him, the pilot said he had to come up with a plan. His immediate need was to stay afloat so he removed his shoes, took off his pants, and got on his back. He even thought of using his credit card from his wallet to reflect the sun and use as a beacon. Though that did not work, he put his white sock on his hand. Eighteen hours later, completely exhausted and without hope, he managed to hold up his hand and attract the attention of a passing yacht.

The good news is Michael Trapp lived to tell the story because even under these extreme, adverse conditions, he had a plan and was able to prioritize how he would execute it. Hopefully, none of us will ever be in a situation this dire, but every day we are faced with situations that require us to problem solve and plan.

What is Planning and Prioritizing?

Planning is the executive function that requires thinking about the future. Planning involves setting an achievable goal and strategically determining the steps required to achieve it. Good planners consider whether they have the resources (time, ability, material, etc) to accomplish the goal. They are also flexible in case they have to change their plan if they encounter an obstacle or if the original plan isn't working out the way they thought it would. Below are six planning steps:

1. Define a goal (what you want to accomplish and when)
2. Decide what you must do to accomplish your goal (steps in the plan)
3. Consider the resources you will need to carry out your plan (materials)
4. Identify what obstacles you might encounter (possible barriers)
5. Determine the order things should be completed (prioritize)
6. Evaluate if your plan is working and be willing to modify it if necessary (flexibility)

Prioritizing is an important part of planning. People prioritize in different ways. Some people like to do the hardest job first while they are fresh and have a lot of energy. Others prefer to tackle the easiest tasks so they complete them and reduce the amount of things they have to do. The order in which you do things may be based on your interests, your mood, or your personal feelings about tasks more than anything else.

Strategy: Evaluate How Well You Plan and Prioritize Schoolwork

At the beginning of this book we asked you to evaluate how well you plan and prioritize. This is a good time to think about how you answered those questions.

- Do you plan how to get your homework and studying done after school?
- Do you enter your assignments into your planner or cell phone?
- Do you prioritize by making and following a list of which assignments to do first, second, etc?
- Do you make and follow a written plan to complete long-term assignments?

Practice Activity: Think More About Planning

If you are not doing as well as you like in these areas, try THINKING more about making plans and setting priorities. During the day, get into the habit of asking yourself questions such as:

- When am I going to do homework or study today?
- Have I written my assignments down?
- Have I thought about what is important to get done today?
- Are there any long term-projects I need to plan?
- Did I make plans to get together with my friends?
- Am I following my plan to save money so I can go shopping?

Practice Activity: Set Planning Goals

Decide what areas of your life you want to plan better (e.g., schoolwork, plans with friends, chores around the house, job responsibilities, plans for a party, etc.). Choose just two or three things to plan so you won't be overwhelmed. You won't be successful if you try to plan too much.

Directions: Look at the list of areas below and select the areas in which you want to improve your planning (use the blank lines to write more areas).

- Saving money for things I want
- Going out with my friends
- Spending time with my family
- Keeping track of my job hours
- Creating a homework schedule
- Setting up a schedule to study for tests
- Starting and finishing long-term projects
- Planning a party for my friend
- Selecting clothes to wear each day
- Buying new books
- Getting directions to places before driving to them
- _____
- _____

Strategy: Writing Your Plan

Sometimes thinking about your plan is not enough. Writing an Action Plan could be more effective. An Action Plan contains a clearly defined goal, steps you will take to achieve the goal, a timeline for accomplishing each step and the final goal, and a method of evaluating progress.

What makes a good Action Plan?

It must be clearly written so it is easy to follow. It must be realistic. If the plan is followed the goal should be attainable. Below is an example of an Action Plan.

Action Plan

Statement of Objective or Goal: I want to earn at least a B+ in American History this semester.			
IMPLEMENTATION		EVALUATION	
What needs to be done?	**By whom and when?**	**How can you tell if you are making progress?**	**Describe how well you are doing.**
Pay attention in class	Me/Daily	After each class, ask myself if I was paying close attention.	I am checking myself a few times during class to make sure I stay focused.
Do required reading	Me/Daily	Track what I read every day and see if I am keeping up with the assigned reading.	I have been writing my reading assignments in my planner and doing them every day.
Get grades of B or better	Me/Weekly	Keep a grade chart of all the grades I get.	I have been keeping a weekly grade chart.
Study for quizzes and test by reading notes and reviewing	Me/A couple of days before the test	Test myself or ask someone in my family or a friend to quiz me.	I am reviewing old exams and tested myself on new material each night.

Practice Activity: Write an Action Plan

Action Plan

Statement of Objective or Goal:			
IMPLEMENTATION		EVALUATION	
What needs to be done?	**By whom and when?**	**How can you tell if you are making progress?**	**Describe how well you are doing.**

Strategy: Prioritizing Your Assignments

It is going to be very helpful to get into the habit of planning and prioritizing your schoolwork, homework, and studying. Start each day by writing down the assignments that you need to complete or tests you need to prepare for. Write the date each assignment needs to be completed (date due), when you will study for a test, and prioritize each task by assigning it a number that will tell you the order in which the task should be done. Look at the sample "GET IT DONE TODAY" chart below to show you how your finished product might look.

GET IT DONE TODAY

Date_____

Priority	Assignment	Date Due	Completed
3	Work on plant life report	3/10	☐
2	Math page 204 prob. 1-25	3/4	☑
1	Social studies quiz *New Deal	3/4	☑
5	Call Mike to review poetry project	3/4	☐
4	Write recall questions-Sci. chapt.7	3/4	☐
			☐
			☐
			☐
			☐
			☐

Practice Activity: GET IT DONE TODAY

Directions: Fill in the blank GET IT DONE TODAY form on the next page.

1. Write all assignments and study sessions for the next week.

2. Decide which assignments must be done immediately and which can be delayed for a while. Determine the due date.

3. Under "Priority," write "1" by the assignment you plan to do first, "2" by the one you will work on second, etc.

4. Check each assignment on your list as you complete it. You will feel accomplished when you see your list diminish.

5. Finally, write any work not completed on the next day's GET IT DONE TODAY list.
   An extra copy of this list can be found in the appendix and can be copied for your future use.

GET IT DONE TODAY

Date_____

Priority	Assignment	Date Due	Completed
_____	_____		☐
_____	_____		☐
_____	_____		☐
_____	_____		☐
_____	_____		☐
_____	_____		☐
_____	_____		☐
_____	_____		☐
_____	_____		☐
_____	_____		☐
_____	_____		☐
_____	_____		☐

Strategy: Planning for Long-term Projects

You will be involved in long-term planning, both in and out of school. For example, your service club is planning to collect canned goods for a local food bank, or you are planning a surprise party for your best friend, or you have a long-term research assignment. All of these require planning and prioritizing, and though the particulars may vary, the process for successfully completing them has a lot in common.

When an assignment isn't due for at least a week or longer:

1. The day you learn of the assignment

   ▪ At school: Write the details of the assignment in your planner.

   ▪ At home:
   Write the assignment on the due date of your calendar, which should be hung in a clearly visible place (on the wall by your mirror; on the fridge in the kitchen…)

   Count how many days you have until it's due

   Divide the assignment into manageable parts and decide what you need to do each day so you complete the assignment at least two days before the due date (leaving the last two days for re-reads and revisions). Plan for any support, such as being driven somewhere and ask for that help today, so your helper can be available. Get what you'll need to complete the assignment: supplies, addresses, emails, phone numbers.

2. Each day after:

   ▪ If the teacher makes any changes to the assignment, note them in your planner

   ▪ Schedule your times to work on the assignment and stick to it.

Strategy: Organizing Your Long-term Research Projects by Setting Goals

When a term paper or research project isn't due for a long time, we tend to put it off until the last minute and then we PANIC! The strategy on the next pages will help you to break large projects down into manageable steps. While it may be tempting to skip steps, if you follow the directions, you will get your work done on time and without stress for you and your parents.

GOAL-SETTING FORM

REQUIREMENTS:

Assignment:

_____

_____ typed: # of pages or words _____

_____ oral: amount of time _____

Format requirements (e.g., double spaced, one inch margins, bibliography page, works cited page):

_____

_____

_____

Other requirements: (e.g., number of sources)

_____

_____

_____

DATE DUE: _____

MY TARGET GRADE: _____

THE PRE-WRITE
STEP 1: Tentative Topics

If you can choose a topic of your own, consider two of interest to you.

1. _____

2. _____

Due date _____   Doing __✔__   Done __✗__

STEP 2: Preliminary Research for Topic Selection

Search the internet, library and other sources to find the one topic that has enough information to fulfill the requirements and is of interest to you.

My topic: _____

Make a list of the sources. Include the titles, pages and where to find the sources with the information you will want to use.

Due date _____   Doing __✔__   Done __✗__

STEP 3: Narrow Topic

If your topic is too broad, skim through your sources for a central theme to help narrow it down.

_____

Due date _____   Doing __✔__   Done __✗__

STEP 4: Brainstorm

Skim again through your sources (if you need to) to come up with as many subtopics as possible. Choose the most relevant ones (at least three).

1. _____

2. _____

3. _____

4. _____

5. _____

6. _____

Due date _____   Doing __✔__   Done __✗__

STEP 5: Prioritize

Decide the order in which you want to present your subtopics (from Step #4). One way is from strongest to weakest.

1. _____

2. _____

3. _____

Due date _____   Doing __✔__   Done __✗__

THE FIRST WRITE

STEP 6: Thesis Statement

Write a sentence that states your central theme and at least three controlling ideas (refer back to the subtopics you wrote in step #4). Your thesis should include what you will say or prove about your topic.

Thesis: _____

Due date _____   Doing __✔__   Done __✗__

STEP 7: Rough Outline

This is a plan for a 5 section paper, but check the teacher's specific requirements.

   I.   Introduction including the thesis statement

   II. Heading (subtopic 1)

   III. Heading (subtopic 2)

   IV. Heading (subtopic 3)

   V.   Conclusion

Due date _____   Doing __✔__   Done __✗__

STEP 8: Note Cards

Read the sources to gather information about "Heading one" of your rough outline. On an index card, write that heading on the top of a note card. Then, write the ideas you find about that subtopic. Unless you are directly quoting, write a paraphrase so you don't accidentally plagiarize.

For each source, copy the bibliographical information on one card. This should include the source title, author, page number, publisher's name, date and place of publication. This will become your paper's bibliography, but be sure to find out your teacher's requirements for a bibliography format. If you have more than one card for the same source, in the upper right-hand corner, write an abbreviation for the source title and author's last name and the page number of where you paraphrased the information.

Bibliography card:

Davis, Sirotowitz, Parker.
Study Strategies Plus
Plantation, FL: Specialty Press, 2012

Note card:

Davis, Sirotowitz, Parker, Study +

To retain about 70%, review notes within 24 hours of taking them. Research proving that practicing retrieval aids memory.

pp. 104-105

Due date _____   Doing __✔__   Done __✗__

STEP 9: Sort Cards

Number cards according to your outline.

Due date _____   Doing __✔__   Done __✗__

STEP 10: Rough Draft

Begin writing your first draft by following your outline. Include any teacher requirements for this draft.

Due date _____   Doing __✔__   Done __✗__

THE HOME STRETCH

STEP 11: Revise

Read your rough draft in its entirety.

Does it prove your points and back them up with facts?	_____ Yes _____ No
Are they in the order you want them to be?	_____ Yes _____ No
Does your paper read easily and fluently?	_____ Yes _____ No
Would anyone reading your paper understand your thesis?	_____ Yes _____ No
Have you checked for grammar, spelling, and word usage errors?	_____ Yes _____ No

Due date _____   Doing __✔__   Done __✗__

STEP 12: Rewrite

Rewrite using your revisions as your guide.

Due date _____   Doing __✔__   Done __✗__

STEP 13: Edit

Ask someone else to check for errors in capitalization and grammar, organization of your sentences, paragraphs, punctuation, and spelling. Make sure that all rules are followed.

Due date _____   Doing __✔__   Done __✗__

STEP 14: Final Copy

Include all visuals and cover sheet, etc.

Due date _____   Doing __✔__   Done __✗__

⊃ **Now ask yourself:**

How will my life be better now that I can plan and prioritize?

1.
2.

Chapter Seven

SELF-MONITORING AND METACOGNITION

> *"Learning is not attained by chance. It must be sought for with ardor and attended to with diligence."*
>
> —John Quincy Adams

These are the skills that will be covered in this chapter.

> Thinking about thinking
>
> Making a plan to learn
>
> Tracking your performance

Jill decided to surprise her boyfriend by making a cake for dinner. It would be the first cake she'd ever baked, but she ate cake, she liked cake, and she knew her boyfriend liked cake. She was in a rush because it was getting close to when he was arriving for dinner. She quickly turned on the oven and began putting the flour, sugar, etc. into bowls. When she looked at the recipe, she read that she needed to add eggs. So, she opened the refrigerator and found an empty egg carton! Her brother had used the last of them for breakfast that morning. She had no way to get to the grocery store, so she was stuck.

If Jill would have paused more often to think about what she was doing she would have made fewer mistakes.

What is Self-monitoring and Metacognition?

Self-monitoring is an executive function that enables us to be aware of how we are acting. Through this self-awareness we can judge ourselves and make appropriate changes in the way we behave.

Metacognition is defined as "thinking about thinking." Metacognitive skills can be applied to learning. These skills involve asking yourself questions that will enable you to plan effectively, monitor your plan to see if it's working, and evaluate the final results of the plan. This can give you the power to use a more thoughtful approach to problem solving that will likely be more efficient and yield higher grades.

Self-monitoring and thinking about how you process and retain information improves learning. Students who believe that their ability to learn can improve over time earn higher grades. They take charge of their learning, set goals for themselves, and feel empowered to achieve more. They use learning strategies (like the ones in this book) to learn better and they become more motivated.

Jill could have asked herself the following questions:

Before baking (Do I have a plan?):

- Have I ever baked cake like this before?
- Do I understand the directions?
- Do I have the equipment and ingredients I need?
- How much time do I need to complete the baking?

Once Jill has thought about what she needs, she can start baking. As she bakes, she needs to monitor how she's doing, just in case she needs to make some changes.

During baking (Am I doing what I need to do?):

- Am I following the directions?
- If not, do I need to get help by calling my mother or looking on-line?
- Do I need or want to make any changes?
- Will I finish the cake on time?

After Jill finishes the baking process, she needs to take a minute to reflect upon how she did, evaluate the outcome and decide whether she would need to change anything to make her next baking venture even better.

After the cake is done (Did it come out the way I wanted it to?):

- Did I finish on time?
- Does the cake look and taste as I expected?
- Are there any changes I would make the next time I bake one?

Notice that Jill's questions never involved specific ingredients. The reason is because metacognitive questions focus upon how something is being done (the process) rather than the ingredients (which in a classroom would be the content or facts).

Practice Activity: Examine Your Behavior

We started this chapter by showing you the mistakes Jill made while baking. She could have been more successful if she paid attention to what she was doing and examined her behavior. She could have asked herself questions before, during, and after baking.

In this activity, you will learn how to generate your own metacognitive questions to improve your learning.

Directions: Check the questions below that will help you plan and do your work before, during, and after you have finished an assignment.

Before you start any assignment, ask yourself if you have a plan. You can ask yourself questions such as:

- ☐ What do I already know about this subject?
- ☐ What do I need to learn?
- ☐ What are the directions/requirements?
- ☐ How will my work be evaluated?
- ☐ What strategies can I use for this task?
- ☐ What is my goal?

During the assignment, monitor your progress. You can ask yourself questions such as:

- ☐ How am I doing; do I understand?
- ☐ What strategies can I use to efficiently and successfully complete the assignment?
- ☐ Do I need to change the strategies I am using?
- ☐ If my strategies aren't working, where can I go for help?
- ☐ Am I staying focused?
- ☐ Am I exerting enough effort to achieve my goal?

After you're done, evaluate how you did. You can ask yourself questions such as:

- ☐ Have I achieved my goal?
- ☐ Have I followed the directions/requirements?
- ☐ What could I have done differently?
- ☐ How does my self-evaluation compare with the grade or evaluation I received from the teacher?
- ☐ Does my grade reflect the effort I put into completing this assignment?
- ☐ How can I use this knowledge to plan for the next task?

Ask yourself these questions every time you have to learn something new or get an assignment. Go ahead and make a copy of these questions, add more of your own and refer to them until you've learned them without looking back.

⊃ Now ask yourself:

How will my life be better now that I ask myself metacognitive questions to monitor how I work and learn?

1.	
2.	

Teachers and Study Coaches: What can you do?

After you have introduced metacognitive thinking and taught students how to ask themselves metacognitive questions, you will want to provide reinforcement and guided practice.

Five strategies to teach metacognitive thinking:

1. Use the KWL chart below to teach metacognition.

   Choose a topic that students are currently working with.

   Guide them to activate, verbalize and then list under the **K** column their prior knowledge about the topic.

   Brainstorm with them so they voice and list what they want to learn about the topic in the **W** column.

   Model questions students can use to monitor their progress as they work on the assignment.

   Model questions students can use to decide and list what they learned in the L column.

   Model questions students can use to evaluate their performance once they complete the assignment.

   They then read their entries in the **K** column to assess whether they were accurate, and correct any that were inaccurate.

K	W	L
What I KNOW	**What I WANT to Know**	**What I LEARNED**

2. Use reciprocal teaching from teacher-to-students and between student-to-student to reinforce how to use metacognition.

3. Use journaling for students to reflect on how they will apply metacognitive questioning in school.

4. Provide opportunities for students to do their own planning and monitoring of how they are learning.

5. Once students seem to grasp the concept of metacognition, brainstorm with them, have them write their own questions, and post them on the board.

⊃ Students can use this skeletal outline for additional independent practice.

Suggested metacognitive questions to ask yourself

Before you start any assignment, determine if you have a plan. Ask yourself the following questions:

1.

2.

3.

4.

5.

During the assignment, monitor your progress. Ask yourself the following questions:

1.

2.

3.

4.

5.

After you're done, evaluate how you did. Ask yourself the following questions:

1.

2.

3.

4.

5.

Chapter Eight

LEARNING STYLES

"Tell me and I'll forget; show me and I may remember;
involve me and I'll understand."

—Chinese proverb

These are the skills that will be covered in this chapter.

> Identifying your preferred learning style(s)
>
> Applying your learning style(s) to your school work
>
> Choosing environments where you learn best

Ms. Jenkins, a high school science teacher, knew that not all the students in her class learned the same way. Edra, for example, liked to work with a few of her friends when she did projects. She seemed to pay attention better and enjoyed the interaction with other students. She had great ideas and was the type of person who could take charge in a group and lead others. Issac, on the other hand, preferred to work alone. In a group he had trouble being flexible and open to other student's suggestions. He'd get disappointed when someone would disagree with him, and he would shut down rather than be open to the other people's suggestions.

Matt thought best when he was at his computer keyboard. It was painful for him to write an essay using paper and pencil. When his fingers "danced" across the keyboard his mind was sharp and alert and his ideas would flow more easily. Jessica liked to make a detailed outline of what she wanted to include in a report before she could even write the first sentence. She had to get a good grasp on the overall message that she wanted to convey, plot it out on paper, and then put her ideas into sentences. Her approach, although different from Matt's yielded similarly good results.

Shandra studied best when she had her ear buds in and her iPod® set to her favorite playlist. She found that she concentrated better with music in the background. It relaxed her and made studying less painful. Tim, however, needed a quiet area to study. If the phone rang or he could hear the television playing in the room next door, his concentration would be broken and he couldn't learn a thing. Instead of being relaxed by background noise or music, Tim found it irritating.

These students learn in different ways. They have their own personal learning style that suits them.

What are learning styles?

A learning style is the way we process and retain information. The three main styles are visual, auditory or kinesthetic. We may also use a combination of two or more, though most people have one style that works best for them.

Visual: Visual learners learn by recalling images in their minds and seeing diagrams. As a visual learner, you might need to keep your surroundings as neat as possible since visual learners tend to feel disorganized if their work area is visually overloaded. Keep materials you need visible since it's hard for visual learners to find what they can't see. According to the University of Illinois Extension, 40 percent of secondary students are visual learners and tend to be good at math.

Auditory: Auditory learners best remember information they heard as poems and songs or in a lecture. They may excel at music and learning foreign languages. As soon as you identify places to file and store your materials, tell yourself where those places are, so that you "hear" the location. That will help you find materials at a later date.

Kinesthetic: Kinesthetic learners learn best with movement (like pacing while studying) and taking things apart (and hopefully putting them back together). They may also enjoy art or repair work. Kinesthetic learners also respond well to writing and drawing, so writing and studying from note cards and taking notes are effective study tools. Keep your school supplies within easy reach, since you will tend to find things that you can "feel." Research results suggest that 50 percent of secondary students fall into the kinesthetic category.

Combination: These are learners who combine learning styles. There is no right or wrong learning style. Learning style also involves the environment in which you learn best. This includes the place, the noise level, the organization of the space and sometimes the colors that surround you. Even your personality affects how you learn and the choices you make to learn in the best ways.

Do the following activities to explore your best styles of learning.

Strategy: Identify Your Personal Learning Style

Below are two easy activities that will help you identify your personal learning style.

Practice Activity #1: What is Your Personal Learning Style?

Choose one person to be the word caller. Everyone else closes their eyes.

Word caller: I am going to say a word. You may close your eyes if it helps you concentrate. When I say the word, I want you to think about what comes to your mind about the word.

The word caller says the word, "cat."

Give everyone a chance to think about it and then each person will tell how he or she imagined the cat.

Some people will see a picture of the cat. Others will hear the cat's purr, while others will describe the soft fur of the cat or imagine the cat jumping on to the furniture. Someone may even have seen the letters, c-a-t.

Practice Activity #2: What is Your Personal Learning Style?

▨ Tell the group to remember a dance, either one they danced or one they attended.

▨ Did you remember the dance because:

1. You watched it?

2. You recalled the music?

3. You danced it?

Practice Activity: Understanding How You Learn Best

People learn using three different learning modalities. A learning modality can be either visual (seeing), auditory (hearing) or kinesthetic (touching or moving). While you may use any one or all of these modalities at certain times, most of us use one modality more often than others. That modality is part of your **preferred learning style.**

Directions: To figure out your preferred learning style, pretend that you have to learn 20 new words and their meanings for a big test. How would you tackle this job? (Check any statements that describe you—you can have none or more than one in any category.)

1. I would prefer to:

_____ read the words and definitions over and over again.

_____ close my eyes and "see" them in my mind.

_____ look at pictures that portray the words and their meanings.

If these are the ways you like to learn new material, you may learn best by seeing, and you are probably a visual learner.

2. I would prefer to:

_____ recite the words and definitions to myself over and over.

_____ have the words and meanings taped and then listen to them.

_____ discuss the meanings with someone.

_____ listen to the teacher's explanations and recall them later.

If these are the ways you like to learn new information, you may learn best by hearing, and you are probably an auditory learner.

3. I would prefer to:

_____ write the words and definitions.

_____ draw pictures that remind me of the meanings.

_____ dramatize the meanings.

_____ move around as I concentrate.

If these are the ways you like to learn new information, you may learn best by feeling and moving, and you are probably a kinesthetic learner.

4. Think of other examples that show whether you prefer an auditory, visual, or kinesthetic learning style and write them below.

_____

_____

_____

If you checked off more than one preference in each modality, it means that you often combine styles to learn. Many people are like you and combine what they see with what they hear and write.

Why is this important? When you know which learning style works best for you, you can take control and use your strongest modality so you can learn most efficiently.

Practice Activity: Apply Your Learning Style to Your School Work

Directions: In the left column, list your core classes and think of the types of tests or projects that are assigned. In the right column, list the learning modality that you believe will work best for you.

Example:	
CORE CLASSES	**BEST LEARNING MODALITY TO USE**
Math	visual + writing
English	auditory + kinesthetic

Strategy: What's Your Best Study Environment

Your study environment can affect your learning. Most people become accustomed to studying in a certain setting, around a certain time of day, and in a specific way. They find that can concentrate best when they are in a comfortable study environment.

Directions: To understand the type of environment in which you study best, answer the questions below.

1. I prefer to study:

    _____ early in the day (even if it means getting up early to study before school).

    _____ soon after getting home from school.

    _____ in the evening.

    _____ at various times, depending on "what's happening."

2. I prefer to study

    _____ with background noise, such as music or television.

    _____ in almost total quiet.

3. I prefer to study

    _____ alone.

    _____ as part of a group.

4. I prefer to study

    _____ in my room.

    _____ in another room at home where my family hangs out.

    _____ at someone else's house.

    _____ at the library.

    _____ other _____

5. On the lines below, write a description of the setting, time of day or night, and whether you prefer studying alone or with others. Explain why and how you think this environment would help you concentrate and study best.

    _____

    _____

    _____

    _____

    _____

    _____

    _____

    _____

⊃ **Now ask yourself:**

How will my life be better now that I have a better understanding of how I learn best?

1.	
2.	

Teachers and Study Coaches: What can you do?

The first goal is to educate students about learning styles and why knowing their preferred styles can help them to learn more effectively.

This is one activity that can be easily done in class.

Practice Activity: Guess My Learning Style

1. Brainstorm to find out what students already know about learning styles.

2. Have students read the descriptions of the four main learning styles at the beginning of this section.

3. Ask students if, based on what they read and may already know, they think they can tell if someone else is a visual, auditory, kinesthetic or combination learner.

4. Ask for a few volunteers to each tell a short story while the class watches for clues to see if they can guess each person's major learning style.

5. If you think the class needs cues, you can suggest that they ask themselves the following questions:
   Does the story teller mention color, shape, size, design of something?
   Does she use her hands to give visual cues?
   Does the story teller imitate sounds or use descriptions of how something sounds?
   Does the story teller act out the story with a lot of movement?

6. Students write down what style they believe each volunteer is and then take a consensus.

After your students identify their personal, preferred learning styles, you need to retain and use this information for differentiated learning. It will also help your students if you inform them that different situations require different study choices.

Traditionally, our understanding of learning styles has been visual, auditory and kinesthetic. However, today, another theory is Neil Fleming's VARK model. According to this model, there are four primary types of learners: visual, aural/auditory, read/write and kinesthetic. You may wish to search online for more information about learning styles and additional inventories.

At this time, there is ongoing research as to the roles of learning styles and the parts they play in the learning process. Suggestions are for teachers to use a variety of presentations that take all modalities into account and teach concepts over a period of time, rather than trying to "cram" a lot in at once.

According to the University of Illinois, only 10 percent of secondary students learn best auditorily, but 80 percent of instructional delivery is auditory. In the classroom, it would benefit all students if your presentation style included visual, auditory and even kinesthetic cues.

Here are some activities and presentations you can try in your classrooms:

For visual learners:

- Graphic organizers such as mind maps or webs
- Diagrams, charts, graphs, and maps
- Highly descriptive words to elicit visual imagery
- Flash cards and notes
- Color coding or other visual highlighting
- Computer graphics
- Cartoons
- Posters
- Text with many illustrations

For auditory learners:

- Small cooperative groups or panels
- Time for students to read out loud to themselves
- Read and repeat
- Short lectures with embedded verbal cues
- Discussions
- Interviewing or debating
- Oral reports

For kinesthetic and tactile learners:

- Field trips
- Role playing and dramatic interpretations
- Doing something physical (such as exercising)
- Associating concepts with actions (e.g., rhythmic movements)
- Time for students to learn by doing
- Drawing
- Playing board games
- Making dioramas
- Making models
- Following instructions to make something
- Teaching how to use note cards

Chapter Nine

COMMUNICATION

> 66 "Perhaps you will forget tomorrow the kind words you say today, but the recipient may cherish them over a lifetime." 99
>
> –Dale Carnegie

These are the skills that will be covered in this chapter.

Using positive behaviors in class

Understanding teacher expectations

Communicating with teachers and asking for help

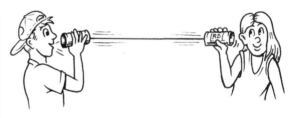

Blake often gets to his world history class late. It's his first class and he's tired, so he lays his head on his desk. He doesn't really like the class, so doesn't participate unless the teacher calls on him. When she does, he sometimes sounds annoyed, mostly because he isn't fully prepared. Blake rarely looks her in the eye. He tells his parents that his teacher just picks on him for no reason.

Sara was a good student in elementary school. In high school, her grades have dropped, and she feels confused. She has six teachers and six different sets of requirements. Sara studies the way she always has, which works well in English class. In science, though Sara wonders from where her science teacher gets the information he puts on his tests. She has no idea!

Jeremy wants friends and does have a few...for awhile. It makes him angry that so many kids just don't get his humor; everyone is so touchy. When one of his new friends has a problem, Jeremy thinks it's no big deal and tells the boy to get over it and stop whining. The next thing Jeremy knows, he's minus another friend.

So what's going on with Blake, Sara, and Jeremy? All three are good kids but are having real issues.

- Blake might ask what he's projecting about himself. Does the teacher think he's disinterested and rude? Wouldn't it be great if we could videotape him so that he could see what his teacher sees? If he's willing to "please" his teacher, Jeremy might feel less "picked on."

- Sara just hasn't realized that all teachers aren't one big blob. Each teacher is an individual with separate requirements, and it's Sara who has to figure out how to study differently for each teacher's class and tests. With a little analysis of her teachers' styles and tests, Sara will be the good student she was back in elementary school.

■ Jeremy wants friends, but his lack of empathy and cooperation alienates them. Jeremy will find people who like to hang out with him once he develops an awareness of how other perceive his communication.

What is communication?

Communication is the process of transmitting information from one person to another. In school, we communicate most often with other students and teachers to share our ideas, needs and feelings. When students and teachers are able to communicate effectively with one another, it enriches the teaching and learning process for both.

Students: What can you do?

Were you ever surprised, as Blake was, that a teacher often seemed offended by or angry with you? You knew you didn't intend anything bad, so why didn't your teacher like you?

Have you felt like Sara? She's not doing well on her tests or quizzes and she can't understand what her teachers expect of her or from where they're getting the information they put on tests.

Did you ever feel that you were trying to be a good friend, but were rejected and you didn't know why? Jeremy is the kid who wants friends, but his style of communication makes him difficult to hang around with for very long.

Do you see yourself in any of these students? Have confidence; with a little work and perseverance, you can overcome any of these downers. First do the activities in this section and then reflect upon the positive changes you can make in your life.

Practice Activity: Think About Teacher-Pleasing Behaviors

How do you want your teachers to behave toward you? Two things you might say are that you want them to treat you fairly and respectfully. What do you think teachers might say about your behaviors towards them? Most say that they want students to treat them respectfully and be ready and willing to learn.

Different teachers have a variety of behaviors they point to as frustrating (sometimes annoying) to them because those behaviors interfere with their teaching.

Directions: Read the following list of teachers' top 10 bothersome behaviors. Check any that would describe your behaviors in class. Then read the matching teacher-pleasing behavior that's in *italics*.

From those behaviors you've identified as yours, choose one and plan to change it. When you feel comfortable with your new and improved behavior, begin to change others one at a time until you're a teacher-pleaser instead of a teacher-pest.

Why would you want to please your teachers? You are a considerate, good person. And also because your behavior may affect your grades!

Student behaviors that bug teachers and 10 student behaviors that please teachers.

1. _____ Not looking at the teacher.

   Establishing eye contact with the teacher shows that you are paying attention. This behavior is considered both polite and important in any situation.

2. _____ Showing up unprepared and not ready to work.

   Arriving in class with appropriate materials tells the teacher that you are responsible and ready for the class. If you find it hard to remember which materials to bring to class, have a checklist of what to bring to each class.

   Preview a new chapter or topic before class so that you have the necessary background to listen for new information.

3. _____ Sitting sprawled, head down on the desk, as if you're sleeping.

   Sitting up and looking alert show that you are ready to listen, participate and take notes. If sitting up for extended periods hurts your back, you may want to discuss this with your parents and get your back checked. If you are tired, either get more sleep at home or consult a doctor about your health.

4. _____ Turning in assignments late, or worse, not turning them in at all.

   Completing assignments by following all directions and turning them in by their due dates means that you are fulfilling your obligations. Be sure to write all details of assignments in your planner, including the due dates. Use the strategies in the chapters Starting, Focusing, and Finishing and Handling Homework, for plans to get homework turned in on time.

5. _____ Coming to class late.

   Coming to class a few minutes before it begins gives you the opportunity to get organized. If you are habitually late, walk to class a little faster, have shorter hallway conversations, and plan ahead so you don't have to make a locker stop before every class.

6. _____ Socializing with friends during classroom instruction.

   Stopping social conversations as soon as class starts shows respect for your teacher and fellow students. Plan to talk with friends before and after class. So your friends don't think you've abandoned them, alert them that you won't be discussing next weekend's plans while your teacher is lecturing. You can blame it on us!

7. _____ Asking questions that have nothing to do with a lesson or have already been answered.

   Participating in class with thoughtful questions and comments means that you are listening carefully to class discussions. Before asking a question, think about whether it is relevant to the lesson or if it's been answered. If you still don't understand, try to phrase your question in a way that lets the teacher know you recognize the issue has been addressed, but you need further explanation.

8. _____ Interrupting when the teacher is busy with other students or other things.

   Waiting until the teacher is free before asking for help is simply good manners. Unless it's an emergency, be sure the teacher is free to speak with you. If you need to have a lengthy discussion, ask if you may meet at another time the teacher has available. Briefly give your reason for needing the meeting.

9. _____ Being rude to a teacher or other student because their opinions differ from yours.

Disagreeing is fine if it is done in a respectful, courteous way. If you are rude, even if your opinion is the right one, you come across as wrong. Listen to others' opinions and when you voice your disagreement, argue about their points, not about their personalities.

10. _____ Doodling or drawing while you need to be listening or taking notes.

Showing that you are ready to listen and participate is good for you and respectful to your teachers. Preview the textbook the night before so that you'll be ready to listen for and note down what is new for you and be able to make relevant comments that add to the class discussions. Having a purpose will help you to participate rather than doodle.

Practice Activity: Reading Your Teachers

If you understand how your teachers teach, what they emphasize, and from where they take information for tests, you can predict what each teacher expects of you.

Directions: Write the name of each of your courses in the "Course" columns. As you go down the list, check the space that best describes how each of your teachers teach and test.

Courses

Teacher's presentation

1. Puts information on a board

2. Presents through lecture with students expected to take notes

3. Initiates class discussion and participation

	1.	_____	_____	_____	_____	_____
	2.	_____	_____	_____	_____	_____
	3.	_____	_____	_____	_____	_____

Homework

1. Assigns for practice only; no grades given

2. Assigns and grades

3. Checks only to see if it's been done

4. Checks and writes comments

	1.	_____	_____	_____	_____	_____
	2.	_____	_____	_____	_____	_____
	3.	_____	_____	_____	_____	_____
	4.	_____	_____	_____	_____	_____

Courses

Test Questions come from

1. Textbook chapters

2. Textbook questions

3. Teachers' lectures and discussions

4. Worksheets, films, labs, etc.

Test Preparation

1. No review given

2. Study sheets handed out

3. Review is done verbally in class

Types of Tests Given

1. Multiple choice

2. True/False

3. Matching

4. Fill-Ins

5. Essays

6. Varies from test to test

1. _____ _____ _____ _____ _____

2. _____ _____ _____ _____ _____

3. _____ _____ _____ _____ _____

4. _____ _____ _____ _____ _____

1. _____ _____ _____ _____ _____

2. _____ _____ _____ _____ _____

3. _____ _____ _____ _____ _____

1. _____ _____ _____ _____ _____

2. _____ _____ _____ _____ _____

3. _____ _____ _____ _____ _____

4. _____ _____ _____ _____ _____

5. _____ _____ _____ _____ _____

6. _____ _____ _____ _____ _____

⊃ Now that you know how to understand your teachers' expectations, you can adapt how you study and focus.

Practice Activity: Communicating with Teachers

Now it is time to communicate better with teachers. The following activity offers suggestions for approaching teachers in constructive ways that elicit positive results. This type of communication can be used in any situation and with anyone.

- You need to discuss something of importance to you. *Begin by saying, "Excuse me, may I speak with you?" Then, briefly tell the teacher why you need to consult and ask what time would be convenient to meet. When you set a time, show respect by being punctual.*

- In advance, decide the points you want to discuss and begin with the most important to you. *You may want to write down the points you want to discuss and refer to them when you meet. This will keep you organized and demonstrate to your teacher that you are serious and thoughtful, as well as respectful of her time.*

- Establish eye contact (but don't stare). *We all appreciate feeling that the person to whom we are speaking is listening. Eye contact shows you are attentive.*

- Be prepared to compromise. *If you and your teacher cannot totally agree, be positive and respectful. If you are reasonable and fair, your attitude will encourage your teacher to also be reasonable and fair.*

Directions: Role play one or more of the following situations. You take one side while another person takes the other side. Then switch sides so you have to recognize and understand both positions.

1. ▨ You are a student who needs to change a topic for a research paper.

   ▨ The teacher is resistant to allowing you to change because he feels that it's a little late to make changes.

2. ▨ You are a student who is asking for extended time to turn in a report.

   ▨ The teacher tells you that there is a due date, and you need to adhere to it.

3. ▨ You are a student who is having difficulty in math and needs extra help.

   ▨ The teacher tells you he has limited time for help sessions.

4. ▨ You are a student who needs a great recommendation written for a college to which you want to apply.

   ▨ The teacher is one who doesn't always seem approachable.

⊃ **Now ask yourself:**

How will my life be better if I communicated more appropriately with others?

1.	
2.	

Teachers and Study Coaches: What can you do?

We know that students want to do well and also want the approval of their teachers. We also know that some of them don't know how to get to that point, mostly due to faulty communication skills. You have the chance to guide them to become better communicators and more empathetic people.

After students complete the communication activities listed above, use role playing and discussions to help them become aware of the possibilities they have to improve their relationships through positive communication. We also suggest that you communicate your needs for their behaviors in specific, helpful language.

What about the student with ADHD, Asperger's, nonverbal disability or behavioral differences?

Though this student can be a challenge, you can definitely help. First, ask parents to share their at-home observations about their child's strengths and needs. Parents often have a wealth of valuable information and the desire to ally with you for their child's benefit. Also, when appropriate, consult with your guidance counselor, school psychologist or other professional who has knowledge of your student and specific strategies and accommodations that would help you to help him succeed in your class. The truth is that all of the strategies presented in *Study Strategies Plus* will help most students regardless of their abilities, skills, and differences.

Parents: What can you do?

You know the mantra: Communication is key. You can be your child's most important role model and mentor, guiding her to understand and apply her preferred ways of learning and appropriate behaviors of cooperation and empathy.

If your child often comes home angry, saying that she's always picked on by her teacher, you need to take an objective view of how your child's behaviors and communication comes across to others.

Read *"Teacher Pleasing Behaviors"* to see what your child's responses were and use it to begin discussions:

- Can she make some positive changes so that a teacher views her as a participating member of the class?

- Can you role play with him to help him understand how to make changes?

- Can you share similar experiences you've had that worked well for you?

If your child often comes home upset about trouble with friends, first determine if this is common teenage drama. If your child will talk with you about his perceptions, try to get a realistic and objective idea of his part in the problem. If, however, you see your child becoming overwhelmed to the point that it is affecting his happiness, it may be time to consult with the school and or other professionals.

What if your child has ADHD, Asperger's, nonverbal disability or behavioral differences?

You are your child's best advocate. You and your child need to meet with your child's teachers to share the information about your child that will allow the school and teacher to understand your child's needs and provide the best services possible.

Chapter Ten

READING COMPREHENSION

❝I would be most content if my children grew up to be the kind of people who think decorating consists mostly of building enough bookshelves.❞

—Anna Quindlen

These are the skills that will be covered in this chapter.

> Active reading
>
> Paraphrasing
>
> Identifying topics, main ideas, and supporting details
>
> Using signal words to identify important information
>
> Previewing content
>
> Learning new vocabulary

Sean hates to read. He finds it boring and tedious. Sean reads fine and his vocabulary is good, but he has to read and re-read his textbook. His mind wanders while he is reading and in order to comprehend the material he has to go back over it. When he has to answer unit questions from the book or on a test, he has no idea what the answers are and he has to look them up—again. He feels like it takes him too long to read a chapter and understand it than it should.

Although Sean knows how to read, he doesn't know how to actively read. He doesn't read with a purpose, or think about what he is reading while reading. He thinks simply reading the words is enough, but what Sean is doing is passive reading. He needs to become an active reader.

What is Active Reading?

Active readers think about what they are reading so their minds don't wander. They pay attention to what they are reading and have greater comprehension of the content. Active readers will often preview the reading selection. They get an overview of the structure and content of the text and what they already know about the topics. This gives them a bird's eye view of the material they will read and study and sets the stage for deeper understanding. They apply strategies that will improve their comprehension and memory of the material. After reading, more successful readers realistically assess their comprehension and continue to apply strategies that increase their understanding. They can then generalize what they've read, the classroom discussions, tests or other academic requirements.

Practice Activity: Are You an Active or a Passive Reader?

You can become a more active, engaged and successful reader by following what active, successful readers do.

Directions: 1. First read the differences between how active versus passive readers approach reading. 2. Check the boxes that apply to you. 3. If you have checked some of the boxes in the Passive Readers column, there are reading activities in this section that will help you become a more active reader.

	Active Readers	**Passive Readers**
BEFORE READING	☐ think about what they already know about the topic. ☐ think about what they need to learn from the reading (set a goal). ☐ know what strategies to use that would aid understanding. ☐ know how a section relates to an entire chapter.	☐ do not think about what they already know about the topic. ☐ read without purpose. ☐ read without a plan to use strategies. ☐ read without previewing.
DURING READING	☐ stay focused. ☐ make predictions about what will happen next. ☐ use strategies as they read. ☐ can identify the topic and main ideas of each paragraph. ☐ can distinguish between details that are relevant and support the main ideas versus the details that are unimportant. ☐ can paraphrase (explain in your own words) the topic, main ideas, and supporting details of each paragraph or section. ☐ use strategies to understand the vocabulary within the reading selection. ☐ realize when they don't understand and switch strategies or ask for help.	☐ are easily distracted. ☐ don't think about what might come next. ☐ read without using any strategies. ☐ have difficulty identifying topics and main ideas. ☐ can't distinguish between details that are relevant and support the main ideas versus the details that are unimportant. ☐ don't summarize as they read. ☐ don't apply strategies to understand relevant vocabulary. ☐ don't know what to do when they don't understand.
AFTER READING	☐ know if they met their goals (and their teacher's goals). ☐ can answer questions that are at the end of the chapter or on a test. ☐ feel their ability to read contributes to why they are getting good grades.	☐ move on without reflecting on any goals. ☐ cannot determine where in the reading test questions come from. ☐ believe their lack of understanding and disappointing grades are due to bad luck or teacher bias.

"Reading is NOT a spectator sport!" — Mary Helen Pelton (1993)

To read with comprehension, you need to identify the topic, the main idea and the supporting details.

Review what you checked in the above chart. Are you more of an active or passive reader?

Practice Activity: Picture Perfect Understanding

Active readers often use illustrations to gain additional meaning about a story.

Directions: Look at the picture on this page. Ask yourself the following questions and consider what's happening in the picture.

- Who or what is the illustration about?

- What is the main idea of what is happening?

- What details in the illustration add to the main idea?

On the lines below, write what you think is happening in the illustration.

_____

_____

_____

You have just taken your first step in learning to paraphrase.

Strategy: How to Paraphrase or "The One Sentence Summary"

Paraphrasing is explaining or summarizing a topic, main ideas, and important details in your own words. Paraphrasing helps us understand what we've read or to check our understanding of something we are studying (because if we cannot paraphrase in our own words, we may not understand as well as we think we do). When taking notes for a research project or essay, paraphrasing helps avoid accidental plagiarism. In addition, paraphrasing helps you remember information. If you cannot paraphrase, you could lose as much as half of the information you just read within a day. Reread the passage until you can paraphrase (explain it in your own words).

Here is an easy way to learn how to paraphrase. Ask yourself these questions about what you've read and combine your answers into a sentence.

Who/What?   Did what?   Where?   When?   Why?

For short reading selections, your paraphrase could be a "one sentence summary." We have written this sentence about the alien from the picture on the earlier page. You will have a chance to practice paraphrasing for the following stories.

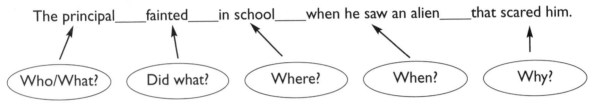

Strategy: Four Steps for Active Paragraph Reading

When you read a paragraph you need to understand the topic, main idea and supporting details. Then, if you can briefly summarize the paragraph in your own words (paraphrase), you will know that you really understand what you've read.

Follow this chart to strengthen your active reading skills.

To Find The:	Read:	Ask Yourself:
TOPIC	title or heading (if there is one). That is usually the topic of the passage. the first two sentences of the first paragraph. That is usually the topic of the paragraph.	WHO OR WHAT is this passage about? WHO OR WHAT is this paragraph about?
MAIN IDEA	the rest of the paragraph.	WHAT is the author telling about the topic?
SUPPORTING	the paragraph a second time to identify the relevant details about the main idea.	WHAT, WHERE, WHEN, WHY and HOW
PARAPHRASE	Think of your answers to steps 1 - 3 (above) and in a sentence or two, say it aloud in your own words.	

Practice Activity: Using the Four Steps Strategy for Active Paragraph Reading

Some of the following paragraphs have their main ideas in either the first or last sentences. That's the most common writing device. A less common placement for main ideas is in the middle of the story, and you'll find some paragraphs with that placement, too.

There are also some paragraphs where authors don't explicitly state main ideas. They put in details and are confident that you will be able to infer what they mean. One way to find the main idea is to imagine a paragraph as a box of "stuff." Then pull out each item (the details) and think about what they have in common. That will lead you to the main idea. Paraphrasing is most helpful for this type of paragraph.

Directions: Use your active reading questions to find the main idea and supporting details of the following short stories. Remember to paraphrase out loud, then write your answers in the chart below each story.

Story 1:

There are new laws in many states directed specifically at teenagers. Some parents and teens are unaware of the new laws, but it is important that they learn about them. Statistics shown that many auto accidents involve teenage drivers. Some of these accidents result in deaths or serious injuries, and often involve innocent passengers of other cars.

When the numbers of these accidents were published, state legislators realized they had to do something to prevent such tragedies. They began devising laws in hopes of saving lives.

The new laws state that teenagers are not allowed to make calls or text while they drive. While some teenagers choose to disobey the laws, most are abiding by them. The reported deaths and injuries due to cell phone calls and texting have dropped dramatically.

Interviews with some teens showed that while they don't all think such laws are either necessary or fair, they obey them because they don't want to pay stiff penalties more than $500.00, do possible jail time or bear the wrath of angry parents. Whatever reasons are for obeying the laws, if it prevents deaths and injuries, the laws are good enough.

Topic:
Main Idea:
Did you find the main idea _____ in the first sentences; _____ in the last sentences; _____ in the middle of the paragraph; _____ was unstated, had to be inferred.
Supporting detail:
Supporting detail:
Supporting detail:
Paraphrase:

Answers can be found in the Appendix.

Story 2:

For centuries, many men attempted to reach the North Pole, but not one succeeded. On September 6, 1909, Admiral Robert Peary claimed that he was the first man to reach the Pole and live to tell about it. However, the family of Peary's personal attendant, Matthew Henson, an African-American, claimed that it was Henson not Peary who had first stepped foot on the site and should be credited with that impressive feat. Peary denied this and he got all the recognition and honors. Interviews with the Inuit men who had been with them for much of the journey seemed to substantiate Henson's claims. They stated that Peary had become ill, may have had frozen toes and was too exhausted to hike the final miles to the Pole. In fact, he rode in a dog sled while Henson marched on and planted the American flag at the site recognized as the North Pole. As further proof, Henson stated in a newspaper interview that, "I could see that my footprints were the first at the spot." There was enough proof of his claim and the U.S. government decided that long-accepted belief that the first man to reach the North Pole in 1909 was Admiral Robert Peary was inaccurate. At age 70, the U.S. awarded Henson the same honors and recognition it had long before bestowed upon his companion, Admiral Peary.

Topic: Main Idea: Did you find the main idea _____ in the first sentences; _____ in the last sentences; _____ in the middle of the paragraph; _____ was unstated, had to be inferred.
Supporting detail:
Supporting detail:
Supporting detail:
Paraphrase:

Story 3:

Welcome to the test center. The rules you must follow are very strict, and we adhere to them. You may not have any books or papers on your desks. You may not have your calculator out until it is time for the math sections, and only the accepted calculators may be used. You must turn off your cell phones and put them away. And, of course, keep your eyes on your own paper or the proctor may think you are cheating and will ask you to leave the room. In addition, your test booklet will be taken and you will be reported to the testing service. We urge you not to break the rules because we do want you to have the best chance of being admitted to the college of your choice.

Topic:
Main Idea:
Did you find the main idea _____ in the first sentences; _____ in the last sentences; _____ in the middle of the paragraph; _____ was unstated, had to be inferred.
Supporting detail:
Supporting detail:
Supporting detail:
Paraphrase:

Story 4:

When we're young, we feel that we will never be old. We like feeling strong and beautiful (and free of wrinkles), but we do get older. Ronald Reagan was elected president when he was 69. Julia Child became a famous chef when she was 51. Grandma Moses didn't learn to paint until age 71, and she then became a celebrated artist. Mick Jagger and Keith Richards of the Rolling Stones, and Paul McCartney of the Beatles, performed in their 60s almost as wildly as they did in their 20s. People who are lucky enough to reach old age say they feel more self confident. Those who continue to be curious about the world, read, learn new things and exercise as much as possible improve their minds even as they age.

Topic:
Main Idea:
Did you find the main idea _____ in the first sentences; _____ in the last sentences; _____ in the middle of the paragraph; _____ was unstated, had to be inferred.
Supporting detail:
Supporting detail:
Supporting detail:
Paraphrase:

Story 5:

We Americans love our pets. In fact, we spend lots of money to keep them healthy and comfortable, pretty and well-clothed. There are studies that show that pets can calm violent prisoners. Other studies and anecdotal records claim that some pets can raise the moods, even lessen severe depression and loneliness of senior citizens, especially those in nursing homes. In fact, animals such as seeing-eye dogs are used for therapy, and as helpers for people with physical and mental disabilities. Some pets are used therapeutically to help people in many difficult circumstances.

Topic:
Main Idea:
Did you find the main idea _____ in the first sentences; _____ in the last sentences; _____ in the middle of the paragraph; _____ was unstated, had to be inferred.
Supporting detail:
Supporting detail:
Supporting detail:
Paraphrase:

Story 6:

Have you ever heard or used the phrase, "people change overnight?" While this may seem true, biologically, it may not actually be the case. It took eons before humans walked upright, shed their thick, hairy fur and gained the ability to create a myriad of sounds with which to communicate. Research has also unveiled the importance genes play in human change, and how long it actually takes before any of those changes become noticeable. Even genes that cause problems often take years to show their effects. For example, someone who inherited a predisposition for diabetes may not get diabetes until late in life. So, the truth is that while some changes might be overnight wonders, most are long-term works in progress.

Topic:
Main Idea:
Did you find the main idea _____ in the first sentences; _____ in the last sentences; _____ in the middle of the paragraph; _____ was unstated, had to be inferred.
Supporting detail:
Supporting detail:
Supporting detail:
Paraphrase:

Story 7:

Cooking a great meal begins with a good recipe, quality ingredients, and superb supplies. You can buy wonderful foods, utensils, and cookware in many stores or online. You can also get a variety of recipes online, use one of your favorites, or be creative and just mix and match ingredients. After deciding what to cook, you need to have everything nearby, ready to cut, chop, measure, and cook. Following the right steps can turn a boring or inedible meal into a gourmet experience. The table should then be set beautifully, and the cooked dish should be presented in a way that is attractive and appealing. You and your guests will be delighted with the results.

Topic:
Main Idea:
Did you find the main idea _____ in the first sentences; _____ in the last sentences; _____ in the middle of the paragraph; _____ was unstated, had to be inferred.
Supporting detail:
Supporting detail:
Supporting detail:
Paraphrase:

Story 8:

A growing number of schools are requiring students to volunteer their time to help those in need. Volunteer experience may include tutoring younger students, visiting the elderly, and working in hospitals. Many students enjoy the experience and volunteer well beyond the minimum hours required. Other students feel that this is an unfair requirement and must be coaxed to complete their hours. However, the people who receive the services are glad the program exists.

Topic:
Main Idea:
Did you find the main idea _____ in the first sentences; _____ in the last sentences; _____ in the middle of the paragraph; _____ was unstated, had to be inferred.
Supporting detail:
Supporting detail:
Supporting detail:
Paraphrase:

Check your answers in the Answer Key in the Appendix. Did you identify the correct main ideas and supporting details? Did you have a paraphrase that captured the gist of the paragraphs?

If you found this activity to be challenging, ask yourself these questions:

- Did I use the **4 Steps for Strategy Active Paragraph Reading?**

- Was there a pattern to my errors? Did I miss more of the paragraphs with the main idea in the _____ first sentences? _____ last sentence? _____ middle sentences? _____ inferred?

- What can I do to improve my skills to identify the main ideas and supporting details?

- If I need help, who am I going to ask?

This skill often requires practice, but it is very worthwhile. You will be able to master it!

Next step...

Do you feel like you're mastering how to actively read paragraphs? If you do, then get ready to apply what you've learned to reading the longer passages and chapters that are in the textbooks and assignments you need for school. Trust us, with your new skills, this is going to be easier than it has ever been. So take a deep, relaxing breath and get ready to read!

Strategy: Identifying Signals in Reading Selections

Authors include certain words and phrases to signal ideas they want to emphasize. When you learn how to recognize and classify those signals, you will also know how to find the information you should study.

Yellow traffic lights signal you to slow down and pay attention to what's ahead. Similarly authors' signals alert you to "shift gears" and pay attention to the information coming up next. A smart reader "obeys the signals" and attends to the facts that follow.

Read the types of signals below and on the following page, then look for them as you read for school. You will then find activities to practice identifying words, phrases, and symbols that authors include as signals in reading selections.

Supporting Signals

The ideas that follow these signals support and extend the ideas that came before the signals.

more

additionally

and

also

likewise

furthermore

moreover

1,2,3,…or one, two, three…

Opposing Signals

The ideas that follow these signals oppose or reverse the ideas that came before the signals.

but

yet

nevertheless

otherwise

although

contrary

not

despite

Definitions

Signals of definitions are not always words, but can be commas or dashes. They may also be appositives or phrases set off by commas to describe the word preceding them.

_____, or _____

Example: His point was trivial, or unimportant to the debate.

_____ appositive _____

Example: The cranium, the skull, houses the brains of most creatures.

_____ – _____

Example: There was such euphoria—elation— felt when the soldiers returned.

Sequence

These words signal the order in which events occur.

now	first
later	second
before	then
after	finally
yesterday	next
earlier	today
last	tomorrow

Superlatives

These words signal something that is "super important" because the facts are unique and don't happen very often. Therefore, they are worth remembering.

"most" words

Example: The most important events for the United States in the 2000s was thought to be 9/11 and the election of President Obama.

"-est" words

Example: The largest building in the world once was the Empire State Building.

Illustrations

These words signal clarifications and further explanations of what came previously.

for example

for instance

an illustration of this is…

a case in point

Main Ideas and Conclusions

These words signal an overall concept or result.

in conclusion	thus
in summary	because
the major point	consequently
as a result	therefore

Absolutes

These words signal information that is often included on true/false tests.

all

always

everyone

never

no one

Presentation Cues

Observe changes in print styles which signal important information.

words in **bold** print

words in *italics*

<u>underlined</u> words

changes in font size or **color**

Practice Activity: Identifying More Signals in Reading Selections

Directions: Read this brief article that has signals in bold type. See if you understand why they are identified as signals and what types of information they signal. Then match the types of signals to the signal words below.

(1) **Most** scientists report that processed food (2) **or** foods that have been canned, frozen, refrigerated, dehydrated or chemically treated, often served in fast food restaurants is bad for our health. (3) **However,** some food that is (4) **first** processed can actually be good for us. (5) **One example** is milk. Milk is pasteurized to kill bacteria. (6) **Before** pasteurization was discovered, many people got sick or died from the bacteria in milk. This processed food is the (7) **best** choice for us to drink. (8) **Likewise,** some fruit juices have been treated to add nutritional value like calcium. (9) **Thus,** we cannot make a blanket statement that (10) **all** processed food is unhealthy for us, since some has been proven to be beneficial.

_____ a.   Superlative   _____ f.   Sequence

_____ b.   Absolute   _____ g.   Illustration

_____ c.   Supporting or additional detail   _____ h.   Sequence

_____ d.   Superlative   _____ i.   Definition

_____ e.   Opposing detail   _____ j.   Main idea or conclusion

Practice Activity: Slow Down and Mind the Signals

Directions:

1. Read the article Hunters and Gatherers.

2. Circle each signal you identify.

3. Check your answers with the Answer Key in the Appendix.

Hunters and Gatherers

All people of long ago had to get food and shelter, just as we do today. However, while we go to the store to buy our food, ancient populations had to rely upon the land. One way that people got their food was to walk around the area picking what grew wild on trees and bushes, such as nuts and berries. Another way was to eat plants and roots that could be dug up. Both of these methods are called _gathering_. While gathering could supply vegetables, nuts and fruits, humans also ate meat. Therefore, the cavemen learned to hunt animals such as deer and rabbits.

Most cavemen got their food by using both methods; they are now known as hunters and gatherers. This was their way of life or their culture. When people develop a culture, they must also devise the tools to maintain that culture. For example, early people created tools that helped them to dig up plants more easily and weapons that allowed them to kill more effectively. As a result of their inventiveness, the early human populations survived and spread their cultures throughout our world.

Answers can be found in the Appendix.

Strategy: Three Sweeps or How to *Really* Read a Textbook

In previous sections, you learned strategies that help improve your reading comprehension by increasing your ability to identify signals, main ideas, and supporting details in paragraphs.

In the strategy we call "Three Sweeps or How to *Really* Read a Textbook," you will apply those active reading skills for longer passages, such as those found in textbooks. The following chart gives you the steps to make reading your textbooks more meaningful.

SWEEP ONE: Preview the Chapter

Previewing before you start reading gives you an overview of what is included in a chapter and its structure.

Preview	What to do
Title	Ask what you already know about the title's topic
Introduction	Read and ask yourself what you think the chapter will be about
Headings & Subheadings	Read to get a general idea of how the chapter is structured; its sequence
Pictures maps and charts	Glance at them – sometimes they help clarify concepts

SWEEP TWO: Read the Study Questions

Reviewing study questions gives you the purpose for reading and an inside track as to the details the author thinks is important and therefore, should be highlighted.

Question beginnings	Look for these details in the question and in the text
Who...?	People
What...?	Events
Where...?	Places
When...?	Time
How...?	Process
Why...?	Reasons

SWEEP THREE: Active Reading

Actively reading heightens your comprehension of the main ideas and supporting details within a chapter. Highlighting (or jotting down notes if you cannot write in your books) is a way to emphasize the important facts and relevant vocabulary. This will allow you to refer back to those facts.

Steps	The Purpose (Why do it?)	What to do
1. **Read the heading.**	To understand the central theme of the section	Think about the theme and how it applies to what you've already learned in previous chapters.
2. **Read the first paragraph.**	To identify the main idea	Think about who or what the paragraph is about.
3. **Highlight the main idea and supporting details in yellow.**	To emphasize only main ideas and supporting details (not interesting but unimportant details) and allow you to easily refer back to them before a test	Ask yourself: What are the main ideas and supporting details in this chapter? Highlight those sentences or jot down notes about them.
4. **Highlight relevant or unknown vocabulary words in a second color.**	To understand a vocabulary that allows you full comprehension of the text	Decide if you need to know the definition of an unfamiliar word or whether you can understand the context.
5. **Paraphrase**	To check whether you really understand the main concepts	After each section, paraphrase the main points in your own words. If you cannot formulate a sentence out loud, you may need to re-read.
6. **Jot brief notes in margins or on sticky notes.**	To act as recall triggers for tests and study questions	Write trigger words or phrases near where they occur in the text, especially if you are unable to write in your textbook.

Practice Activity: Using the Three Sweep Strategy to read an article about King Henry VIII of England.

Directions: Read the following story about Henry VIII while referring to the **Three Sweep Strategy** chart. Write your thoughts in the lines below each step to practice this strategy and become a more active, efficient reader.

Sweep One: Preview

After previewing, I think this chapter will be about:

_____

_____

_____

Sweep Two: Read the study questions

Read the study questions and highlight or underline the details each beginning word asks about. (For example: **Where** was the *Catholic Church* located?)

Study Questions:

1. Who was Catherine of Aragon?

2. What were some of the reasons Henry wanted to divorce Catherine of Aragon?

3. Where were both queens executed?

4. Discuss some of the obstacles to Henry's divorcing Catherine.

5. Why was it important that Henry's wives give birth to a male child?

6. How was Henry's bloodline finally passed on to stay monarchs of Britain?

After reading the study questions, my purpose for reading King Henry VIII is:

_____

_____

_____

KING HENRY VIII

Historical heads of nations are usually remembered for their leadership abilities or their military conquests. However, when we think of Henry the eighth (Henry VIII), the British king of England, we usually think of his six wives! It isn't just because Henry was a serial husband, but more because his private life changed the course of English history in terms of its politics and official religion. Henry's life could have been a script for a television show, but instead was a real life drama for an entire country.

Reasons and Obstacles

The drama begins soon after Henry married his first wife, Catherine of Aragon. Henry married Catherine, his brother's widow, soon after his reign began in 1509. After a few years, Catherine lost many children at birth or infancy until she delivered a girl, Mary. However, Henry blamed Catherine for producing no male heir, which is the only way a royal family continues its line, and decided to divorce Catherine. Furthermore, it seems that Henry had become interested in Anne Boleyn, a maid of honor at his court. One major obstacle to Henry's marrying Anne was that he was still married to Catherine, and he was Catholic. Being Catholic meant that divorce was not allowed, even for a king. Henry asked the Pope, the head of the Catholic Church, to annul his marriage to Catherine. He claimed that his marriage had been wrong (unholy) because he never should have been allowed to marry his brother's widow. Henry's claim was a bit hypocritical since it was he who demanded that the church set aside its misgivings and bless his union to Catherine. To Henry's intense furor, the Pope refused the king's request.

SWEEP Three: *Really* **Read**

Paraphrase the main idea of Reasons and Obstacles:

_____

_____

_____

Solutions

Henry was determined to leave Catherine anyway, so he began to take steps to solve his problem. First, he declared that the Pope had no authority over England. Then, he secretly married Anne Boleyn, even though this marriage was not legally recognized. Henry next kicked out the current archbishop and instead appointed Thomas Cranmer to be the highest church official in England, the Archbishop of Canterbury. Henry then ordered Cranmer to convene a court to rule on the status of Henry's marriage to Catherine. Conveniently, the Archbishop ruled that Henry's marriage to Catherine was null and void. He also pronounced that Henry's marriage to Anne was legal. Can you tell to whom Cranmer owed his loyalty (and his job)?

SWEEP Three: *Really* **Read**

Paraphrase the main idea of Solutions:

_____

_____

_____

Parliament Passes The Acts of Separation

Finally, believing that his marital problems were settled, Henry demanded that The British Parliament pass the Act of Separation. This important act finalized England's break from the Catholic Church of Rome. It also established the Anglican Church as the official Church of England. (Guess who became the head of the church? If you guessed Henry, award yourself an "A") Since the Church of England allowed divorces, Henry had solved his personal problems and at the same time, changed England's state religion forever.

SWEEP Three: *Really* Read

Paraphrase the main idea of Parliament Passes The Acts of Separation:

_____

_____

_____

Henry's Six Wives and What Happened to Them

What about the rest of Henry's love life? He annulled his marriage to Catherine—which is like divorcing her by saying their marriage never really existed and married Anne. Ironically, Anne had a girl, not the right gender to satisfy Henry. So, Henry had a problem again: how would he get rid of Anne? His solution: to charge her with infidelity. Though she vehemently denied his charges, Henry was the king. Therefore, Anne soon was sent to the prison in the Tower of London and executed by having her head chopped off.

Jane Seymour became queen number three, and to Henry's delight, gave birth to a boy. But, soon after producing the long-awaited male heir, Jane died. Not one to linger in grief, Henry immediately married Anne of Cleves, a German princess. Henry soon had that marriage annulled and because she didn't fight him, queen number four left with her head still attached and some money to keep her in tiaras.

Conveniently, Henry's last two wives were both named Catherine. Wife number five, Catherine Howard, was accused of adultery and like her cousin Anne Boleyn, was beheaded. Catherine Parr, wife number six, not only outlived Henry, but had persuaded him to pass a law allowing daughters to be eligible to ascend the throne. So, even though he divorced and killed queens who bore him no male heirs, he finally could rest in peace knowing that his family would maintain its hold on the throne of England, even if it was through the females who would become England's queens.

It is now easy to understand why this fascinating man still remains an imposing figure in history, just as he was during his life.

SWEEP Three: *Really* Read

Paraphrase the main idea of Henry's Six Wives and What Happened to Them:

_____

_____

_____

Practice Activity: Really Reading and Understanding Your Textbook

Directions: Select two highlighters: one yellow and one another color.

Actively read the following passages using the **Three Sweep Strategy** and answer the study questions following each passage.

Steve Jobs: Genius of Our Time

Steve Jobs "exemplified the spirit of American ingenuity." — President Barack Obama

Steven P. Jobs, known around the world as Steve Jobs, died on October 5, 2011 at age 56. Though his health had been questioned for almost seven years, his death seemed to shock people, for whom Steve Jobs, cofounder of Apple, seemed almost invincible.

The Early Years

Jobs was born in San Francisco on February 24, 1955 to Joanne Carole Schieble, an American graduate student and Abdulfattah Jandali, a graduate student from Syria. When his parents decided that they needed to put him up for adoption, they insisted that the parents be college graduates. A lawyer and his wife were due to adopt him, but when Steve was born, they backed out because they wanted a girl. Paul and Clara Jobs, neither of whom had graduated from college, became Steve's adoptive parents, but only after swearing to Ms. Schieble that they would send Steve to college. Throughout his life, Steve referred to the Jobses as his "real" rather than his "adoptive" parents.

Mr. Jobs credits his father Paul with introducing him to electronics, and when he was very young, he built many do-it-yourself projects. While putting together one of those projects, he telephoned William Hewlett, the co-founder of Hewlett-Packard. Mr. Hewlett spoke with the eighth grade boy for 20 minutes, got the parts Jobs needed and arranged to meet him. After meeting Jobs, Hewlett offered him a summer intern job.

At Homestead High School, while taking an electronics course, Jobs met Stephen Wozniak. They became friends based on their mutual interests. Mr. Wozniak's mother showed him an article about "phone phreaks," hobbyists who were illegally breaking in to the nation's phone system. Jobs and Wozniak were fascinated that this could be done, and though Jobs was still in high school, and Wozniak a college freshman, they set out to build and sell their own "blue boxes," devices that were used to make the free, though illegal, phone calls. The boys made $6,000.00 and were on their way.

Jobs enrolled at Reed College in 1972, but left after one semester. Jobs' explanation as to why he dropped out of college was that Reed was very expensive, and he felt that his parents were wasting their savings on sending him there since he had no direction in his life. However, after dropping out, he became a "drop-in," auditing classes that he enjoyed, such as calligraphy. He also slept on his friends' dorm room floors, got free meals once a week at the Hare Krishna temple and made money by returning cola bottles to collect the 5-cent deposits.

The beginning of his career

In 1974, Jobs left his job at Atari (a game software company) to travel to India. He had been interested in learning more about Eastern religions since his free meals with the Hare Krishnas. Upon his return, in the late 1970s, Jobs found that Wozniak had designed what would become the original Apple I® computer. In 1976, the two men invested $1,300.00 of their own money to start Apple®. Wozniak was the technical partner while Jobs would become the marketing partner. It was at this point that Jobs realized that the "dots" of his life were starting to connect. The calligraphy course had taught him to recognize and appreciate taking the time to create beauty. So, he knew that he wanted any computer he and Wozniak produced to be beautiful and to have fonts that were attractive. Before that, no one equated computers with aesthetics, nor did they think about font styles. He also began to realize that it was important to follow his heart rather than paths that other people set for him.

In 1977 Apple® introduced the Apple II® and by 1989, Apple® was in the Fortune 500 with sales of over $600 million. In early 1979, Jobs visited the Xerox® research center where he saw their prototypes for personal computers that would use a mouse. "It was one of those apocalyptic moments," Mr. Jobs said. "I remember…just knowing that every computer would work this way someday…It didn't require tremendous intellect. It was so clear." Jobs knew he wanted to market a mouse to the general public, so he and his team at Apple® developed one that cost $20 to produce, rather than the $1,000 it was costing Xerox®. This led to the creation of the Macintosh®.

Apple® and more

Though the introduction of the Macintosh® caused a stir, its sales were disappointing, and the Apple III®, as well as an office computer named *Lisa*, were dismal failures. After what is often reported to be major and vociferous battles, Apple® laid off 1,200 employees and took away Jobs' control of the company. In 1985, Jobs left Apple®, but often said that he had been fired. Jobs then started a new company, NeXT® and bought Pixar®, a struggling graphics company owned by filmmaker, George Lucas. NeXT® did not succeed, but after Pixar® released the film, "Toy Story," the Disney company bought Pixar® and made Jobs a billionaire.

Twelve years later, Jobs rejoined Apple® at a yearly salary of one dollar as well as an agreement for Apple® to buy NeXT®. In 2001, Apple® released the iPod® and then, in 2007, Apple® put the iPhone® on the market, successfully competing with other smart phones by having a touch screen. Jobs pushed the company into the digital music business with iTunes®, which changed how people bought and listened to music. In 2010, the iPad® was released and 3 million sold within the first 80 days. Then, in 2011, Apple® introduced the iCloud®, taking music storage into a new era. As of this article, no one is sure how this innovation will change culture again.

Though Jobs never graduated from college, in 2005, he was invited to give the commencement speech at Stanford University. In that speech, Jobs stated that being fired was the key to his success. At the time, it was terribly difficult for him, and he felt that he was a failure. Then he realized that though he was rejected and publicly humiliated, he still loved what he did and now he had nothing to lose. He could become "a beginner" and take risks because he already knew what it meant to fail. He told students to never give up or settle, but to keep looking until they found their passion because that's when success is possible. His motto was, "Stay hungry; stay foolish." He was hungry to learn and innovate; he was foolish enough to take risks, be silly with his wife and children and enjoy what the world had to offer.

Even after he knew he was dying, he continued to be involved in Apple's projects, gathered his closest family and friends to tell them how much they meant to him, and basically designed his own end so that it had as much beauty and personal fulfillment as possible. Upon his untimely death, Apple made this statement: "Steve's brilliance, passion and energy were the source of countless innovations that enrich and improve all our lives. The world is immeasurably better because of Steve."

Study Questions:

Think about the Steve Jobs article and answer these questions.

1. Who founded Apple with Steve Jobs?

_____

_____

2. Why did Jobs quit college after only one semester?

_____

_____

3. How did auditing a calligraphy course become central to how Jobs developed his future products?

_____

_____

4. What major idea for future products did Jobs gain from his visit to Xerox?

_____

_____

5. When did Jobs first become a billionaire?

_____

_____

6. Where did Jobs get a summer intern job and how did that occur?

_____

_____

7. What do you think that Jobs meant when he told Stanford University graduates to "Stay hungry; stay foolish?"

_____

_____

Answers can be found in the Appendix.

Volcanoes

Where does the word "volcano" come from?

The word "volcano" comes from Vulcan, the god of fire in Roman mythology, who lived on Vulcano, an active volcano on the Aeolian islands in Italy. Vulcan was thought to be a blacksmith to the gods; he was able to melt and shape iron. Romans believed that the lava and dust of the erupting volcanoes were the thunderbolts sent out by Vulcan from his forge for Jupiter, king of the gods, to throw in battle.

Locations

Volcanoes are not found everywhere on earth (or on other planets and moons). In fact, they exist only in specific places at or near the edges of tectonic plates. Tectonic plates, or irregularly shaped slabs of solid rock, are generally composed of both continental and oceanic lithospheres. However, as solid and massive as they appear, there are cracks in these plates which allow melted rock to rise up to the surface and form volcanoes. Many volcanoes are found along the edges of the Pacific Plate in Japan, Alaska, Central America, South America, and Indonesia. These locations form a circle on the global map, and together they are known as the "Ring of Fire."

Composition

There are two common features that all volcanoes have below the surface: magma and the chimney. Magma is molten rock within the Earth's crust. The chimney, or pipe, is the passageway that carries the magma to the Earth's surface. These chimneys may be just a few miles below the surface, though some chimneys are hundreds of miles deep. The magma they carry is a pool of melted rock and gas that pushes toward the surface. As the magma rises, gases are released which may cause an explosion that expels the magma through the Earth's surface. When the magma erupts, it is called lava. Although from seeing movies, we think of lava as thick and slow moving, it can also be thin and fast moving. Lava can be more than 2,100 degrees Fahrenheit, and the hotter it is, the yellower it appears. After lava cools and hardens, it is known as basalt, which is black in color.

Volcanoes in the United States

In the United States of America, Hawaii has many volcanoes, but Mauna Loa, on the Big Island, is the largest volcano on Earth. The ocean around Hawaii is tens of thousands of feet deep, and tons of lava pile up to protrude from the ocean and form the islands that comprise Hawaii. Mauna Loa's base is 70 miles wide, and its total height, above and below water is almost 6 miles. This means that Mauna Loa is taller than Mount Everest. Though Mauna Loa is the tallest, Mount St. Helens in Washington state is our most active volcano, and unlike mountains, active volcanoes are able to grow taller over many years. Does Mount St. Helens have the potential to grow even taller than Mauna Loa?

Study Questions:

1. What causes volcanoes to erupt?

_____

_____

2. What is the "ring of fire?"

_____

_____

3. Why do volcanoes exist only in some areas?

_____

_____

4. What is the difference between magma and lava?

_____

_____

5. Do you think that Mount St. Helens has the potential to grow taller than Mauna Loa? Explain the reasons for your answer.

_____

_____

Answers can be found in the Appendix.

Strategy: Vocabulary Development

"The difference between the right word and the almost right word is the difference between lightning and a lightning bug."

—Mark Twain

Have you ever read an assignment and just didn't get it? Have you ever been able to pronounce and read the words in a foreign language passage (e.g., Como esta usted?), yet have no idea what the meaning is?

The reason is that even though you can figure out the words, you don't understand the meaning behind the words. Understanding the meaning of the words we read is absolutely vital to comprehension.

Social studies, science, English, and foreign language classes have many words with meanings that you need to learn. The next strategies will enable you to learn and remember new vocabulary for a long time.

Vocabulary Strategy One: The Index Card Method

1. On the front side of a 3x5 index card, write the word to be learned.

2. Look at the word.
   a. Is there a smaller word within the new word that looks familiar to you?
      or
   b. Is there part of the word that sounds like another word that's already familiar to you?
      In our example, we recognized the familiar small word, *APE*, inside the new word, *apex*.

3. In our minds, we then "see" a picture of our APE and associate it with the new word's meaning, *"at the highest point."*
   We then imagine our ape climbing to the highest point of a mountain (and if you can, also imagine the ape doing something silly, like throwing bananas down at people on the lower points).

4. On the back side of the card, write the definition at the top and a sentence that uses the definition in your association *"The ape climbed to the apex of the mountain."*

5. Finally, if you want, draw a picture of your association.

6. Use your visualization and its association with the meaning when you study.

Index Cards

Word

APEX

Front

(Definition) highest point

(Sentence) An ape climbed to the apex of the mountain.

Back

Vocabulary Strategy Two: The Notebook Paper Method

1. Label a section of your notebook for vocabulary.

2. Draw a line down the length of a page about one-third in from the left.

3. Write the vocabulary word in the left column.

4. Write the definition and any examples to the right of the line.

5. To study, fold the right side of the page so it covers the definitions, but leaves the vocabulary words exposed, then test yourself on the words.

6. Review daily and include words from previous tests once a week. You will be able to recall these words, especially if you use them in conversations and writing.

		Subject_____
		Chapter_____
1. word	definition, example, explanation, etc.	
2. word	definition................	
3. word	definition	

Vocabulary Strategy Three: Linking Words and Pictures Method

1. Read the vocabulary word and its meaning.

2. Draw a picture that will associate the meaning of the word. Make it as funny a picture as you can and give it some action, if appropriate. Don't worry about your artistic abilities; just have fun with this exercise.

HEARTY

large and satisfying

GORY

bloody, horrible to see

BELLIGERENT

warlike, ready to fight

DOGMATIC

stubborn

Practice Activity: Learning New Vocabulary

This activity will help you learn and retain new vocabulary, especially if you keep it to test yourself at regular intervals, even after a vocabulary test.

Directions:

- Write words unfamiliar to you in the "WORD" column.
- Write your own definition based upon context and prior knowledge in the "MEANING" column.
- Write the real meaning from a dictionary or computer in the "MEANING" column. (Consider possible multiple meanings.)
- Write the sentence from the text or make up your own sentence in the "SENTENCE" column.
- Write a personal clue by either drawing a picture or making an association with a song, etc. that you know in the "PERSONAL CLUE" column.

WORD	MEANING	SENTENCE	PERSONAL CLUE
isolationist	Your guess: cowards Real: One who opposes the involvement of a country in international alliances, agreements, etc.	From text: In spite of the attack, isolationists still resisted entering the war. Yours: Isolationists don't want to be involved in the affairs of other countries.	The U.S. is isolated by a fence around it.
	Your guess: Real:	From text: Yours:	
	Your guess: Real:	From text: Yours:	

99

WORD	MEANING	SENTENCE	PERSONAL CLUE
	Your guess: Real:	From text:	
	Your guess: Real:	From text: Yours:	
	Your guess: Real:	From text: Yours:	
	Your guess: Real:	From text: Yours:	
	Your guess: Real:	From text: Yours:	

⊃ **Now ask yourself:**

How will my life be better now that I am a more active reader?

1.	
2.	

Teachers and Study Coaches: What can you do?

Reading Comprehension

We often assume that students enter middle and high school with reading skills that allow them to use the textbooks and outside readings for the high level of content required. Sadly, this assumption is sometimes misguided. In this chapter, students practice the most basic skills of identifying the topic, main ideas and supporting details of what they read.

You can introduce these strategies as whole class, teacher-directed, activities. Like all skills, reading instruction needs to be scaffolded. After providing adequate modeling and guided practice using the activities here, guide your students to directly apply what you've taught to their textbooks and outside readings utilizing cooperative learning groups and paired learning. The goal of this additional practice is for students to become independent, active readers.

While we recognize that teaching these basic skills to your students is time consuming, the payoff is well worth both the time and the effort.

Vocabulary acquisition

Many studies have concluded the following truths when teaching vocabulary:

1. Opt to teach a fewer number of words aiming for a deeper level of understanding.

2. Expose students to multiple meanings of words that can be used in various situations, not just on a test.

3. Find ways to repeat words you've taught, preferably in a variety of contexts throughout the semester.

4. Present vocabulary in multiple formats, such as dramatic or role play, associations, illustrations, songs, poems or rhymes.

5. Teach students the two methods of learning vocabulary and provide practice time for them to internalize them into their study habits.

Chapter Eleven

SUMMARIZING AND NOTE TAKING

"Not everything that counts can be counted, and not everything that can be counted counts."

—A sign in Albert Einstein's office at Princeton University

These are the skills that will be covered in this chapter.

> Summarizing
>
> Using different ways to take notes
>
> Including main ideas and supporting details in notes
>
> Using cues to identify important information
>
> Using abbreviations in note taking
>
> Turning notes into study sheets
>
> Combining information from all sources in notes
>
> Frequently reviewing notes

Juan had just read the first chapter of one of Mark Twain's stories. Juan wrote a very long summary, and when he turned it in, he felt good that he had included everything he remembered that was in the story. When Juan received his grade, he was disappointed and so were many of his classmates. His teacher had written that Juan had not summarized, but had included too much information. What? What did that mean? What could he have left out and how could he have told the difference of what was important versus what wasn't? Juan was confused, and his teacher realized that many of the students didn't know how to summarize.

What did Juan need to know to write a summary closer to his teacher's expectations? How does Juan determine what information to include or omit from a lecture or readings to then use for notes, reports or essay tests?

Matt is a student who also had difficultly taking notes. In fact, Matt wrote every word his teacher said. When he had a research assignment, he wrote down every word he read about his topic. When it was time to take a test based on the teacher's lectures or use his notes to write about his research topic, Matt didn't know where to begin.

Both Juan and Matt suffered from information overload. They couldn't separate important from unimportant information when taking notes.

What is note taking?

When we take notes, we write down pieces of information that we have heard, usually from a lecture, or seen, often from a film. When we refer to taking notes (or note taking) we refer to taking those notes in a systematic way so that we will be able to understand the gist of what is important at a later date. Taking accurate notes is a very important skill in school, and it is also in many careers.

Strategy: Summarizing

Summarizing means consolidating key main points of what you have read, seen, or heard. These often include the main ideas and relevant supporting details.

Practice Activity: Summarizing

Directions: Read the selection "Ice" then fill in the box below.

Ice

Everyone has encountered ice in their lives. Depending upon where we live, some of us encounter lots of ice, even walking down the street, while others only encounter it in their cold drinks. But have you ever thought about what ice really is?

Ice is a crystalline inorganic solid and is considered a mineral. The physical properties of water and ice are controlled by a weak formation of hydrogen bonds between adjacent oxygen and hydrogen atoms. Ice appears white or transparent and is brittle, unlike water.

When most liquids freeze, the solid form of their liquid sinks to the bottom. However, when water freezes, its solid form, ice, floats to the top. You know this from your observations of ice cubes in a water glass. You also know about icebergs and glaciers sticking out of the water. And we even know the story of the ship, Titanic, that hit the floating iceberg and sank. The reason for this is that water expands when it freezes, so ice is actually lighter than water and has a gravity that is less than water's. Therefore, ice floats.

Water freezes at 32 degrees Fahrenheit, but if you add an impurity, such as salt, the freezing point lowers. When this happens, it needs to be colder than 32 degrees for the water to freeze and turn to ice. This is why we salt roads and walkways in places where temperatures drop low enough in winter for it to snow. If you live in such a climate, you've probably seen both cars and people "slip-sliding away."

Another interesting point involves ice skaters. Ice melts under pressure, so the pressure of skates causes a thin top layer of ice to melt, and therefore, the ice skaters are actually gliding on water. So the next time you ask for ice in your water glass, put on non-slip shoes to walk down an icy street or wear ice skates to glide over ice, take an extra second to consider the composition of ice.

Topic:
Main Idea:
Supporting Details:
Summary:

Answers can be found in the Appendix.

Practice Activity: Tweet-a-Friend

When you tweet (or text or whatever the newest technology is right now) you should communicate in as few characters as possible. Consider that restriction as you summarize.

The scenario:

You've decided to run for president of your school. You believe that you have many great ideas that would help improve your school. You wrote up what you believe and submitted it to the student government. Now you have to summarize everything you said so you can tweet it to the students in 25 words or less.

Directions: Read the topic and details, then write the main idea. Finally, write your tweet in 25 words or less.

Topic: Why you should vote for me!

Main Idea:

Details about me:

I am honest and kind. I am in advanced classes and work hard to get good grades. People say that I have leadership qualities, and I think I know how to persuade people to help me. I am comfortable speaking to teachers, the principal and peers, and I have spoken in front of audiences at school.

Our school needs to get students more involved. I'd like to start a student panel where kids who get into minor trouble could bring their cases and tell their sides. The members of the panel could help mediate. For instance, if two kids were fighting, the panel could help make peace between them. We need to extend our lunch time and have more variety in our choices of food. We need to begin planning for homecoming and proms, and I have some ideas for creative events that would keep fees low so that more of us could afford to attend.

Tweet (25 words or less):

_____ _____ _____ _____ _____

_____ _____ _____ _____ _____

_____ _____ _____ _____ _____

_____ _____ _____ _____ _____

_____ _____ _____ _____ _____

Strategy: Simple Outlining

To take notes from a textbook, you need to include only the most important information. Using the Simple Outlining strategy you will be able to arrange that information in an organized way so that you can quickly identify the main ideas and supporting details.

Before you begin taking notes, you'll need to identify the topic, main ideas and supporting details. Then you're ready to "simply outline."

1. Refer to the sample outline below.

2. The section or chapter title of a reading will be the title of your outline.

3. Headings or topics are indented and identified by Roman numerals (I, II, III, IV, etc.).

4. Subheading or subtopics are main ideas. They are indented and designated by capital letters (A, B, C, D, etc.).

5. Supporting details are indented and designated by Arabic numerals (1, 2, 3, 4, etc.).

6. Sub-details are designated by lower case letters (a, b, c, d, etc.).

Once you practice a while, this is a simple way of organizing your notes.

TITLE

I. Heading
  A. Main idea
    1. Supporting detail
    2. Supporting detail
      a. Sub-detail
      b. Sub-detail

  B. Main idea
    1. Supporting detail
    2. Supporting detail
      a. Sub-detail
      b. Sub-detail

Practice Activity: Simple Outlining

Directions: Read and highlight the text on the following page, "Pompeii, the City That Slept for 1,500 Years." Then prepare a simple outline on the form below.

Title

Pompeii, the City That Slept for 1,500 Years

I. Heading/Topic
   Eruption

   A. Main Idea

      1. Supporting detail

      2. Supporting detail

   B. Main Idea

      1. Supporting detail

      2. Supporting detail

      3. Supporting detail

      4. Supporting detail

      5. Supporting detail

      6. Supporting detail

II. Heading/Topic
    Discovery

    A. Main Idea

       1. Supporting detail

       2. Supporting detail

B. Main Idea

   1. Supporting detail

      a) Sub-detail

      b) Sub-detail

      c) Sub-detail

   2. Supporting detail

      a) Sub-detail

      b) Sub-detail

III. Heading/Topic
     City Now Alive

     A. Main Idea

        1. Supporting detail

        2. Supporting detail

     B. Main Idea

        1. Supporting detail

        2. Supporting detail

Answers can be found in the Appendix.

Pompeii: The City That Slept For 1,500 Years

Imagine a major city, built on a mountain, bustling with 20,000 people. Now, hear a violent explosion of a volcano long dormant within that mountain. As your picture changes from one of life to one of death and destruction, would you assume that immediately after the eruption ceased, people would rush to unearth the treasures of that city? Believe it or not, no one disturbed that city, Pompeii, for the next 1,500 years! Today you will learn about the disaster of Pompeii and its remarkable aftermath.

The Eruption

However, Pompeii was built upon the hardened lava of a past volcanic eruption of Mt. Vesuvius in Italy. Its citizens seemed unaware of the potential for disaster. They built mansions, traded and enjoyed their lives in that picturesque setting.

In 79 A.D., this dormant, or inactive, volcano erupted again. First, an explosion sounded loudly enough to be heard for miles. Next, lava cascaded down the mountain onto the lavish homes of Pompeii. Then, ash and pumice stone covered the city, followed by a fierce electrical storm that diminished daylight. Gaseous fumes then killed any remaining life. Finally, in the days after the eruption, rain hardened the pumice stone and ash and buried the city under 18 feet of crust.

The Discovery

In 1748, when excavations of the ruins of Pompeii finally began, the preservation was the most remarkable of its time. Remains of 2,000 of the 15,000 Pompeians who had perished were found in near-perfect condition. The ash cover had hermetically sealed, kept out oxygen and other decaying elements, from Pompeii for more than 1,500 years. Not only were intact skeletons found, but evidence that the catastrophe took them by total surprise was also discovered. For instance, eggs lay unbroken, jugs held still drinkable wine, and on dining tables, half-eaten meals remained untouched on their plates. The remains of people were found in various stages of action, most certainly surprised at what was befalling them. One example was a woman and her daughter holding one another in what would prove to be their last tight embrace. An example of misguided priorities was a man discovered standing with his arm outstretched, holding a sword. He had one foot on a pile of gold and five men laying at his feet. It was concluded that he had slain the men and was threatening a sixth while defending his wealth, even as he himself was dying.

A City Alive With People Once Again

Today, Pompeii is again a bustling city. Sixty percent of the ruins have been excavated and restored, and its treasures, both tangible and historical, continue to be uncovered. The magnificence of Pompeii intrigues and draws millions of visitors from around the world. People live on the slopes of Mt. Vesuvius. This time, though, its citizens not only know of its history, but also know that another eruption is possible. However, we can feel confident that if another disaster were ever to occur, it will not lay uncovered for 1,500 years. With our ability to get anywhere at any time within hours or via the Internet, in seconds, any disaster would be uncovered almost before it ends.

Strategy: Mind Mapping

Drawing mind maps for notes can be fun and allow you to picture in your mind how supporting details relate to main ideas. Then, when you take a test, you only have to capture the image you took to remember the details. There are many maps you can make. It all depends upon which pattern works best for you.

Before you begin taking notes, you'll need to identify the topic, main ideas and supporting details.
Then you're ready to mind map.

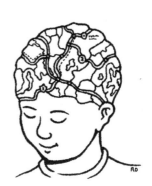

1. Write the subject or topic in the top middle of the page and circle or box it.

2. Under the topic, write each main idea that relates to that topic.

3. Draw one line from the topic to each main idea.

4. Write the details that support each main idea.

5. Draw a line from each main idea to its supporting detail.

The figure below is only one pattern. You will find others on the following pages, but be creative and draw your own maps. Then practice using them to "see" the relationships that help you understand concepts from your own textbook or outside readings.

Sample Mind Map

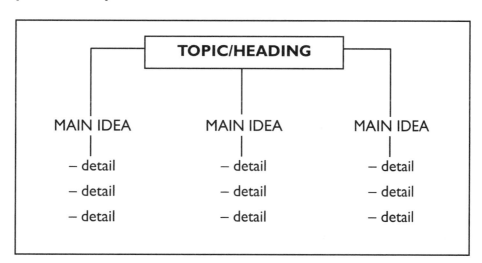

MIND MAPPING MADNESS

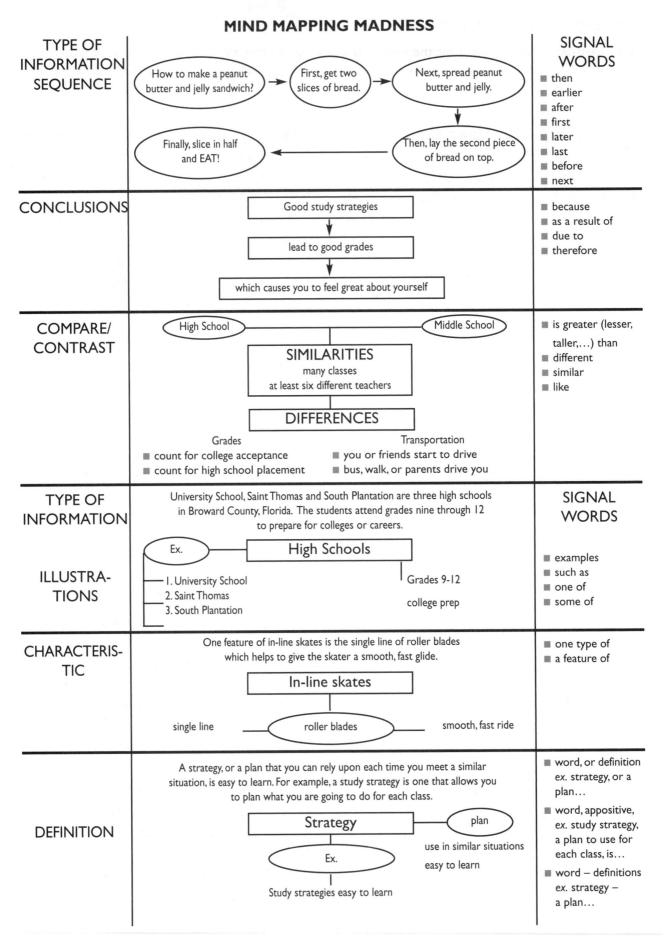

TYPE OF INFORMATION		SIGNAL WORDS
SEQUENCE	How to make a peanut butter and jelly sandwich? → First, get two slices of bread. → Next, spread peanut butter and jelly. ↓ Then, lay the second piece of bread on top. → Finally, slice in half and EAT!	■ then ■ earlier ■ after ■ first ■ later ■ last ■ before ■ next
CONCLUSIONS	Good study strategies ↓ lead to good grades ↓ which causes you to feel great about yourself	■ because ■ as a result of ■ due to ■ therefore
COMPARE/ CONTRAST	High School — Middle School **SIMILARITIES** many classes at least six different teachers **DIFFERENCES** Grades — Transportation ■ count for college acceptance ■ you or friends start to drive ■ count for high school placement ■ bus, walk, or parents drive you	■ is greater (lesser, taller,…) than ■ different ■ similar ■ like
TYPE OF INFORMATION	University School, Saint Thomas and South Plantation are three high schools in Broward County, Florida. The students attend grades nine through 12 to prepare for colleges or careers.	**SIGNAL WORDS**
ILLUSTRA-TIONS	Ex. — High Schools 1. University School Grades 9-12 2. Saint Thomas 3. South Plantation college prep	■ examples ■ such as ■ one of ■ some of
CHARACTERIS-TIC	One feature of in-line skates is the single line of roller blades which helps to give the skater a smooth, fast glide. In-line skates single line — roller blades — smooth, fast ride	■ one type of ■ a feature of
DEFINITION	A strategy, or a plan that you can rely upon each time you meet a similar situation, is easy to learn. For example, a study strategy is one that allows you to plan what you are going to do for each class. Strategy — plan Ex. use in similar situations easy to learn Study strategies easy to learn	■ word, or definition ex. strategy, or a plan… ■ word, appositive, ex. study strategy, a plan to use for each class, is… ■ word – definitions ex. strategy – a plan…

Practice Activity: Mind Mapping

Directions: Read and highlight the following article. Complete the Mind Map on the following page.

The Brain

What does brain size actually mean?

Though an elephant's brain or whale's brain weighs much more than a human brain, scientists say size doesn't count. Instead, scientists compare how much space the brain takes up in comparison to the size of the body it inhabits. For example, an elephant's brain takes up only 1/10,000 of its body weight. The human brain takes up much more space; therefore, scientists concluded that the proportion of a brain to the amount of space it takes up, rather than mere size, is really what indicates how intelligent we are.

What is the structure of the human brain?

The brain looks like a large gray mushroom with many folds, called convolutions, on its surface. The brain consists of three main parts: the cerebrum, the cerebellum, and the medulla oblongata.

The cerebrum is the largest part of the brain. It lies in the upper region of the skull. Its surface has many deep convolutions and the deepest furrow actually divides the cerebrum into two halves. These halves are called the right and left brain hemispheres. The cerebellum lies in the rear of the skull, just behind the cerebrum. The medulla oblongata, at the top of the spinal cord, connects the brain with the spinal cord that runs down the back of the human skeleton.

What are the brain's basic functions?

Our brain controls all of our bodily functions. It is the transmission and receipt of messages by the various parts of the brain that allow us to perform these amazing actions.

The cerebrum controls our five senses, determining whether and how we see, hear, taste, smell, or feel. The hemispheres of the cerebrum are truly remarkable because the right hemisphere controls the left side of the body while the left side controls the right side. This means that if you are right handed, the left hemisphere of the brain is more dominant for you. Many people believe that left-brained people are highly verbal with better math and logic skills while right-brained people have great imaginative and creative abilities. Thus, the cerebrum plays a major role in our lives.

The cerebellum has important functions as well. It allows us to move smoothly instead of in jerky spurts. It also controls our balance. A dancer's or an athlete's coordination and agility can be attributed to the intact functioning of the cerebellum.

The medulla oblongata controls our basic life functions such as the involuntary movements of breathing or heartbeats. It also controls our reflexes like sneezing or a quick response to avert an accident. If the cerebrum and cerebellum stop working, a human may survive strictly due to the continued functioning of the medulla.

How else is the brain important to our lives?

Each region of the brain serves a specific purpose and affects specific functions. Damage to the brain, such as from a head injury, results in loss of the skill the affected area controlled. However, research has proven that if one area is impacted, another area often takes over the job.

It used to be thought that as a person aged, the brain diminished until it barely functioned, often referred to as senility. It has been proven that although the brain does shrink in size, we can exercise our brains by using mnemonics, continuing to learn new skills and having new experiences. Even reading and doing crossword puzzles seem to keep our aging memories sharp.

The brain controls every aspect of our thinking, feeling, and behavior. A computer may beat the human brain in speed or the total amount of information it can retain, but it is the brain that is the most intricate and amazing creation known to man.

Mind Mapping

The Brain

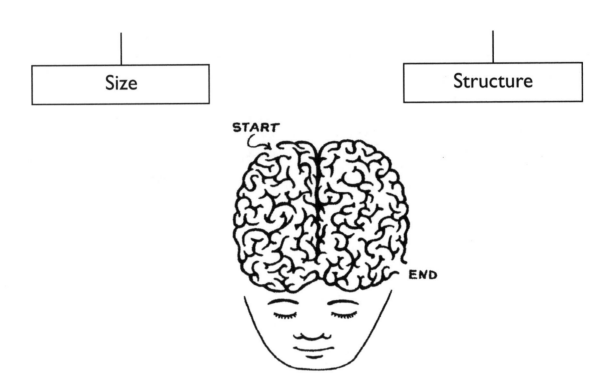

Size

Structure

HOW DOES THE BRAIN CONTROL BEHAVIOR?

Function

Importance

Answers can be found in the Appendix.
See if you can find your way through the "brain maze" from start to end.

Strategy: Combo Notes

Combo notes is a method that is quick and easy to use. It combines the organizational benefits of simple outlining with the visual images of mind mapping. It also gives you the freedom to develop your own symbol system to emphasize the main ideas and supporting details. A big advantage is that you can use it while you listen to lectures and won't need to rewrite or reorganize later.

First, you'll need to read and identify the topic, main ideas, and supporting details. Then, you're ready to combo.

1. Write the topic or title in the top center of the page and circle.

2. Write the first main idea on the next line, beginning at the margin and box.

3. Indent and write the supporting detail, then star it.

4. Indent further and write the sub-detail using a different symbol for it.

5. For clear organization, keep the margin alignment consistent and skip lines between main concepts.

Sample Combo Notes:

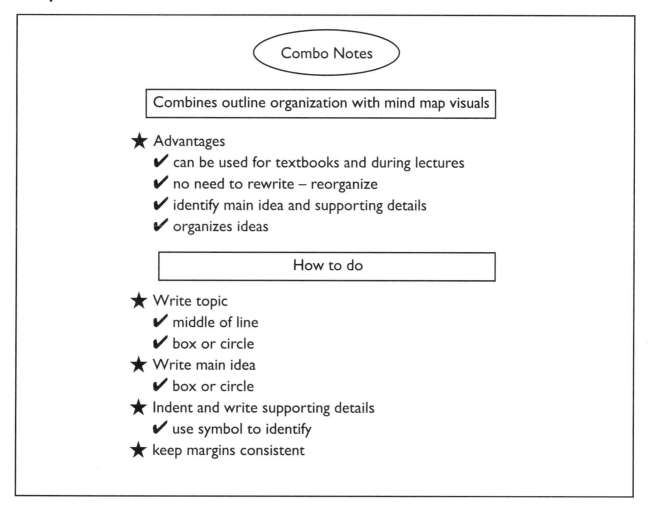

Practice Activity: Writing Combo Notes About King Henry VIII

Directions: You read about King Henry VIII when you learned the **3-Sweep Reading Strategy**. Go back to the highlighting you did for that story and use this skeleton form below to write "combo-notes" about Henry.

Taking Combo Notes

Henry VIII

Henry VIII's private life changes English religious history

Henry seeks to divorce first wife Catherine of Aragon

★ Reasons
   ✗ _____
   ✗ _____
   ✗ _____

★ Obstacles
   ✗ _____
   ✗ _____
   ✗ _____

★ Solutions
   ✗ _____
   ✗ _____
     ✔ _____
     ✔ _____

Parliament passes Act of Separation

★ _____
★ _____
   ✔ _____
   ✔ _____

Henry's six wives and what happened to them

1. _____
  ★ _____
2. _____
  ★ _____
3. _____
  ★ _____
4. _____
  ★ _____
5. _____
  ★ _____
6. _____
  ★ _____

Answers can be found in the Appendix.

⊃ **Some additional note taking tips:**

■ Write brief notes on sticky notes and put them next to the text to which it refers in a textbook or notebook. You can also stick it on your desk as a quick reference.

■ Write your notes on index cards, then file them in an 4x6 or 5x7 index card file box. This is an efficient organizational filing system useful for exam preparation.

Strategy: Identifying Cues That Signal Important Information In Lectures

Teachers lecture for about 85% of class time. When your teacher lectures, it pays for you to listen. Why? Because what a teacher says will include main ideas and details that will (probably) be answers to a homework assignment or on your next test.

Your question might be how you can determine which facts from a lecture are the important ones. The answer is that lecturers use three types of cues. If you pay attention to the statements that follow these cues, you will know which information to learn.

1. VERBAL CUES

The same signal words that authors use in textbooks are used by lecturers to cue you to information they believe is important. Refer back to the reading comprehension chapter for a reminder of those signal words and their meaning.

2. PRESENTATION CUES

While a textbook uses bold type or italics to signal important information, a lecturer may emphasize importance by

■ saying certain words or phrases slower, faster, louder or softer.

■ repeating key words or phrases.

■ spelling out words.

■ writing key concepts on a board.

3. BODY LANGUAGE (NON-VERBAL) CUES

If the lecturer changes the pace or movements of arms, hands, head or body, it may be your signal to note what's being said because it's important. Study each teacher's usual pattern of speaking and moving. When you notice an exaggeration or change of style, you will recognize that the teacher thinks this part of the lecture is important enough for you to write it down.

Practice Activity: Identifying Cues To Important Information

1. Directions: Watch a television newscast. As you watch, fill in the verbal, presentation, and body language cues the speaker is using.

Newscast channel and/or speaker _____**Date:** _____

Cues:

Verbal: _____

_____

_____

Presentation: _____

_____

_____

Body language: _____

_____

_____

2. Directions: For one day, closely observe your teacher's lecture cues. As you listen and watch, write down the verbal, presentation, and body language cues you see.

Class and/or speaker _____**Date:** _____

Cues:

Verbal: _____

_____

_____

Presentation: _____

_____

_____

Body language: _____

_____

Strategy: Taking Great Notes From Lectures

A lecture is your teacher's gift to you. Why? The teacher has done all the work by researching the entire subject, culling out the most important main ideas and details and is presenting them to you in the form of a lecture. Listen attentively to lectures, but unless you take accurate notes, you're wasting the gift.

Caution: Additional but important details may be in your textbook. Be sure to read it and then add any new facts to your notes.

Before the lecture:

- Preview your textbook chapter the night before so you'll know what to focus on during the lecture.

- Decide which style of note taking to use: outline, mind map or combo.

- Review abbreviations you can use for speedier writing.

- Pay attention to what's being said and to any cues.

During the lecture:

- Only write down what you don't already know.

- If the teacher's talking fast and you're writing slow, practice writing and listening at the same time.

- If the teacher's speaking style allows, listen, then write a paraphrase (in your own words).

- Abbreviate and don't write the small words (e.g., a, and).

- Skip lines between each concept and write one idea per line.

After the lecture:

- Read your notes within 24 hours of taking them.

- Correct any inaccuracies.

- Fill in any missing information.

- Get together with classmates to pool notes and check that yours are accurate and understandable.

- Jot down questions to ask your teacher or classmate if you don't understand something in your notes.

- You'll find specific strategies for using your notes for review and practicing retrieval.

Some questions about difficulties in taking notes:

- **What if I get lost along the way and miss some of the information?**
  Skip a few lines, tune back in to the lecture and after class, ask the teacher or a classmate to explain it.

■ **What if I can't understand something the teacher said?**

Write a large question mark in the left margin and after class, try to find an explanation in your textbook or online. If you can't find it, ask a classmate or set up an appointment to see the teacher and ask for clarification.

■ **What if I have a diagnosed learning difference, and I can't take legible or accurate notes?**

First, practice taking notes with the goals of being able to take them yourself. However, if this is impossible, then speak with your teacher about allowing modifications, such as getting the teacher's notes ahead of time, getting a classmate's notes copied for you or getting permission to tape lectures. If you can receive accommodations, be extra diligent about learning the information from those notes.

Strategy: Using Abbreviations To Take Faster Notes (Speeding Legally)

Remember Matt? He wrote too much, and it was a chore that took him too long. When you summarized, you used as few words as possible. When you text or tweet a friend, you use abbreviations. You already have the skill to abbreviate when you take notes.

Additional Abbreviation Tips:

1. Use key words and phrases rather than complete sentences.
2. Leave out "little" words that don't add to recall, such as "a," "the," "to," "in," etc.
3. Leave out vowels; btwn (between); smpl (simple or sample).
4. Make up your own abbreviations and practice using them.
5. When you use a new abbreviation, print it and its meaning at the top right corner of the page, then box it in, so you quickly see it.

Abbreviations For More Effective Note Taking:

Symbols

#	number
%	percent
$	money, dollars
+	plus, and, more, also
−	negative, not, no, none
=	equal
≠	unequal, doesn't equal
>	greater than, more than
<	less than, smaller than
≥	equal to or greater than
≤	equal to or less than
è	to or toward
ç	away from
±	about, more or less
@	at, per, each
∴	therefore

A few letters only

Amt	amount
Assoc	association, associate
b/c	because
bio	biology, biography
cont	continued
def	definition, define
eg, ex	for example
etc.	etcetera, also, and so forth
govt	government
info	information
intro	introduction, introduce
pp	pages
re	regarding, about
s/t	something, sometimes
w/	with
w/o	without

Strategy: Writing Recall Questions From Your Notes And Using Them To Study

The easiest way to understand what recall questions are is to think of the game, Jeopardy. In Jeopardy, you are given the answer and have to figure out the question. Your notes give you the answers and you make up the questions. The terrific thing about Recall Questions is that this is exactly what your teachers do when they make up their tests. This means that when you use this strategy, you could find that your questions are very similar to the questions your teachers have included on your next test. Moreover, research continues to prove that if you do something with your notes within the first 24 hours after taking them, and periodically review them, you have a much better chance of remembering the information later. If you do this, you will be prepared for pop quizzes and cramming will be a thing of the past! This is also a strategy that alleviates stress.

Here's what your notes could look like when you do Recall Questions. However, while we prefer using this style because it leaves you plenty of room, you could write your questions on sticky notes and place them to the left of your notes:

Practice Activity: How To Write Recall Questions

To write recall questions:

1. Read the first facts in your notes (which you should have written using only the right-hand pages). Think of them as the answer to a test question.

2. Think of questions for that answer beginning with who, what, where, when, why and how.

3. On the left-hand page of your notebook, across from the first facts, write your first question about those facts. As you gain proficiency, you will only need to write key words to trigger your recall.

4. If you will need to recall more than one detail, write that numeral and circle it.

5. Read the next concept in your notes and repeat steps 1 - 4.

⟳ If you take notes from lectures and textbooks, skip enough lines so you have room to add new information.

There are great reasons for you to take accurate notes, but only when you do something with them. The old adage "Use it or lose it" is true for taking notes. If you do something with your notes, you'll remember the information. If you don't, you won't. One painless way to make your notes work for you is to turn them into super study sheets. This is a strategy that we call "recall questions."

Note Taking: Recall Questions

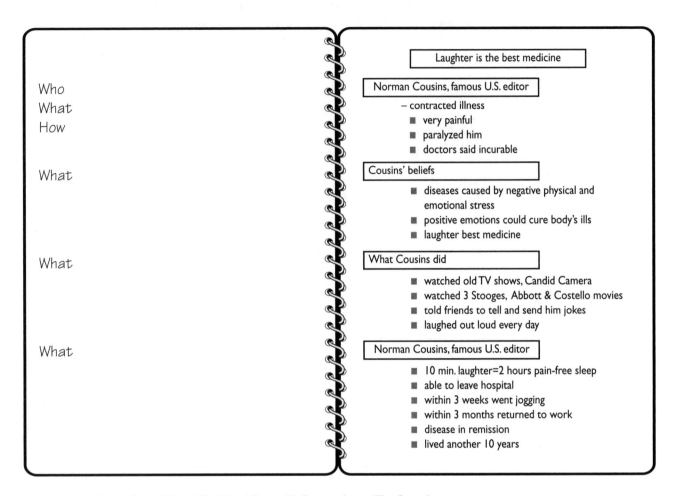

Who
What
How

What

What

What

Laughter is the best medicine

Norman Cousins, famous U.S. editor

– contracted illness
- very painful
- paralyzed him
- doctors said incurable

Cousins' beliefs

- diseases caused by negative physical and emotional stress
- positive emotions could cure body's ills
- laughter best medicine

What Cousins did

- watched old TV shows, Candid Camera
- watched 3 Stooges, Abbott & Costello movies
- told friends to tell and send him jokes
- laughed out loud every day

Norman Cousins, famous U.S. editor

- 10 min. laughter=2 hours pain-free sleep
- able to leave hospital
- within 3 weeks went jogging
- within 3 months returned to work
- disease in remission
- lived another 10 years

Practice Activity: How To Use Recall Questions To Study

Directions:

1. Select a set of notes you have recently taken.

2. Write recall questions on these notes.

3. Use your recall questions to study.

Strategy: Frequently Review Your Notes

Below are the most important reasons that students should review notes frequently.

1. You retain much more when you review your notes within the first 24 hours after taking them and at regular intervals. The chart below, from James Cook University in Australia, says it all!

2. Teacher-directed notes are big clues to what will be on a test.

3. Reviewing notes means you won't have to relearn the material all over again right before a test.

4. Reviewing notes saves study time later.

5. You've made the effort to do all that writing, why waste that?

Strategy: How To Review Your Notes

Review your notes about a week after you've taken them.

■ Use the recall questions you wrote to quickly test yourself on the key points.
If you know the answers (can paraphrase them out loud) without looking back at your notes, you have the information in your long-term memory. If you don't answer correctly, re-read your notes.

Weekly review aids recall and also serves as pre-reading for the teacher's next lecture. It activates your prior knowledge about a subject before being exposed to new material.

It should take you about 10 - 20 minutes per subject to review, but can eliminate hours of re-learning.

⊃ **Now ask yourself:**

How will my life be better now that I can summarize and take notes better?

1.	
2.	

" The lecturer should give the audience full reason to believe
that all his powers have been exerted
for their pleasure and instruction. "

– Michael Faraday

Teachers and Study Coaches: What can you do?

Summarizing is a daunting task for some students. Ask yourself what prerequisite skills your students need to summarize:

They need to be able to:

1. attend to verbal information without significant distraction.
2. retain details in their memories accurately enough to transfer it to notes.
3. comprehend well enough to identify main ideas and supporting details.
4. understand context and vocabulary.
5. decide what information to delete, substitute and keep.

If any of these skills are lacking, you will need to address those areas before you teach or expect students to summarize effectively.

By scaffolding and differentiating your lessons, you can aid most students to attain this skill with proficiency. You can find descriptions of these and other summarizing strategies in *Classroom Instruction that Works* by Robert Marzano, Debra Pickering and Jane E. Pollock *(Copyright 2001)*:

Rule-Based Summarizing Strategy
Summary Frames
Narrative or Story
Topic-Restriction-Illustration (T-R-I)

Not all middle school students have experience taking notes, either from lecture or text. Therefore, even high school teachers may need to explicitly teach how to take notes.

Give a brief lecture about your current lessons. This will be the best starting place since you can control the situation:

Before your lecture and note taking lesson, ask yourself:

■ Do my students have the prerequisite skills to take notes?
  – Adequate hearing and vision
  – Adequate graphic-motor abilities
  – Adequate auditory attentional abilities
  – Grade and age appropriate receptive vocabulary
  – Grade level reading comprehension

■ Do I need to provide accommodations for those students with special needs?

■ Is my lecture well-organized?

■ Am I building in enough verbal cues?

■ Am I modeling?

■ Have I broken down and communicated the specific steps of how to take notes?

■ Do I have a plan to assess whether they understood and have the tools to begin to independently take notes?

During your lecture and note taking lesson, ask yourself:

- Am I using non-verbal and verbal cues for my students?

- Is my presentation style engaging enough to keep their attention?

- Is the content of my lecture of interest?

- Am I allowing enough time for students to listen and write?

After your lecture and note taking lesson, ask yourself:

- Did I hold most of students' attention?

- Am I providing enough practice for students to become independent?

3 Steps to Teach Note Taking

1. Model: Provide a simple outline with main ideas and supporting details filled in.

2. Guided Practice: Hand out a simple outline with only main ideas listed, so students fill in supporting details.

3. Independent Practice: Students to fill in an entire outline, but still receive your immediate, constructive feedback.

- Once students seem to understand the note taking process:

   – Introduce various formats for note taking with the goal being that students will use those that suit their learning styles and the situation.

   – Model how to merge notes from lectures with information from textbooks or outside readings.

Chapter Twelve

MEMORY FOR BETTER GRADES

"Be careful about lending a friend money. It may damage her memory."

—Anonymous

These are the skills that will be covered in this chapter.

Understanding the three types of memory

Using different techniques to memorize

Using efficient ways to study and review

Recalling information for tests

Keisha was determined to do better in her American History class. She read the assigned chapters in her textbook, highlighted the main ideas and supporting details, paraphrased out loud and wrote recall questions on the left side of her notes. But she never looked at them again…until the night before the test when she "glanced over her notes."

You guessed the outcome. Keisha was so disappointed when her grade was barely a C. She was devastated, since as she told her Mom, "I worked so hard!"

Keisha did work hard, but then she dropped the ball. The follow-through step that Keisha left out was to review by testing her recall of her notes. Not once, not twice, but the day she took the notes, perhaps a few days later, and again the week after that. If a test wasn't being given for a while, then Keisha would want to review even a month after taking those notes.

This section will help you learn how to get enough information from the printed page, into your head and onto a test.

You will:

1. Learn how your memory works,

2. Learn how to build review into your daily study schedule,

3. Recognize that understanding + remembering + retrieving = learning,

What are Three Types of Memory?

At this time, researchers, psychologists and educators seem to agree that we can categorize memory into short-term, working and long-term, each with its own specific functions.

Memory Type	What it is	How it works
Short-term memory	Temporary storage of information we get from visual, auditory or tactile input. We can store between 4-7 pieces of information for no longer than 20-30 seconds.	You hear or see a phone number. You will remember that number for about 20-30 seconds.
Working memory	Temporary storage of information that we have retrieved from our short-term or long-term memory that we can organize or do something with. All problem solving is done in the working memory.	You want to remember this phone number, then walk across the room, need to find your cell phone and punch in the number. You've solved the problem.
Long-term memory	Continuing storage of information. We may not realize that it's there, but we can retrieve it into our working memory when we need it.	You want to remember a phone number for future use. You repeat it to yourself several times or practice one of the memory techniques that aid recall.

Strategy: Using Memory Techniques

◼ Use the memory techniques on the next pages to organize and commit information you need to recall for tests into your working, then long-term memory.

Review to Retrieve

Why do all this work only to get test scores that disappoint? Remember the phrase, "Use it or lose it?" It's actually true and supported with research:

◼ According to the results of early research done by German psychologist, Hermann Ebbinghaus, unless we review within 24 hours of taking notes or reading, we lose about 80% of what we have learned within one to two days.

◼ Jeffrey D. Karpicke, an assistant professor of psychological sciences at Purdue University who studies learning and memory stated, "Our new research shows that practicing retrieval is an even more effective strategy than engaging in elaborate studying. [By testing recall, there can be] 50 percent improvement in long-term retention…"

Strategies for Storage and Retrieval
You need to:

1. Be attentive to your surroundings.

2. To move information from short-term to working memory, write relevant things down (if you need to). Don't try to remember too much at one time.

3. Underline, diagram, draw pictures, ask yourself questions about what you need to learn to retain information better.

4. To move information from long-term memory, back to working memory practice retrieval (test your recall) rehearse (perhaps with a study partner).

Here are techniques that you can use to enhance your memory.

MEMORY TECHNIQUES

Strategy: Acrostics (silly sentences)

This is a mnemonic device that groups facts into a meaningful sentence. The sentence is usually short and simple.

Facts: To memorize the planets in their order from the sun.
Mercury; **V**enus; **E**arth; **M**ars; **J**upiter; **S**aturn; **U**ranus; **N**eptune

Sample acrostic: **M**y **V**ery **E**ducated **M**other **J**ust **S**erved **U**s **N**achos

Facts: Learn how living things are classified and divided into groups.
Kingdom; **P**hylum; **C**lass; **O**rder; **F**amily; **G**enus; **S**pecies

Sample acrostic: **K**ing **P**lays **C**hess **O**n **F**at **G**orilla's **S**tomach

Facts: Memorize the order of mathematical operations.
Parentheses; **E**xponents; **M**ultiply; **D**ivide; **A**dd; **S**ubtract

Sample acrostic: **P**lease **E**xcuse **M**y **D**ear **A**unt **S**ally

Facts: Learn the countries of Central America.
Belize; **G**uatemala; **E**l Salvador; **H**onduras; **N**icaragua; **C**osta Rica; **P**anama

Sample acrostic: **B**ig **G**irls **E**at **H**ot **N**achos (with) **C**hili **P**eppers

Practice Activity: Make Your Own Acrostic

Directions: In the space provided below, write a list of facts that you would like to remember and write an acrostic to help you remember the facts on this list.

Facts: _____

_____

Acrostic: _____

_____

Strategy: Acronyms (wacky words)

You can use an acronym to help you remember facts. An acronym is a "wacky word" that is created from the first letter of each fact.

Facts: Memorize the colors in a spectrum.
Red; **O**range; **Y**ellow; **G**reen; **I**ndigo; **V**iolet

Acronym: **Roy G. Biv**

Facts: Memorize the Great Lakes.
Huron; **O**ntario; **M**ichigan; **E**rie; **S**uperior

Acronym: **HOMES**

Practice Activity: Make Your Own Acronym

Directions: Create your own acronym (wacky word) about facts you want to remember.

Facts: _____

_____

Acronym:_____

_____

Facts: _____

_____

Acronym:_____

_____

Strategy: Using Charts to Improve Memory

Charts are terrific when you need to compare and/or contrast ideas, characteristics, theories in literature, history science, math, etc. When you test yourself, you can also recall the look of the chart and retrieve it during a test.

For example, you can classify vertebrates according to their common attributes as seen below.

VERTEBRATES

	Blooded	**Breathing**	**Reproduction**
FISH	Cold	Gills	External
AMPHIBIANS	Cold	Gills, lungs	External
REPTILES	Cold	Lungs	External
BIRDS	Warm	Lungs	External
MAMMALS	Warm	Lungs	Internal

Practice Activity: Create a Chart to Help You Remember Information

Directions: In the space provided below, create a chart that will list information that you need to remember. Divide your chart into rows and columns so all the information is organized in a systematic way.

Strategy: Making Important Facts Stand Out to Improve Memory

Highlighting, circling, boxing, starring, and underlining information that you want to emphasize is a great way to improve your memory of significant facts.

Practice Activity: Identifying Important Facts

Directions: Cut out an article from a local newspaper and use highlighting, circling, boxing, starring, and underlining to identify the important facts in the article.

Strategy: Grouping Information Into Chunks to Improve Memory

Grouping information (chunks) is a practice that is used to help remember things. For example, when you have to remember a phone number, you may group parts of the number of the number (area code), then the first three numbers, then the last four numbers. Most people would probably not chunk a phone number of 10 digits into two groups of five.

Practice Activity: Grouping Information Into Chunks

Directions: Think of some examples of information that you could group together to improve your memory.

Strategy: Using Visualization to Improve Memory

We remember things we hear, see, smell, taste, and touch. We can use visual memory (things we see) to improve our recall of facts. We do this by creating images (pictures of words, diagrams, mental images, etc.) that serve as prompts or cues. If you want to remember the students in your math class, for example, you could visualize each row of desks and then using this image write the names of each student. Or, if you are giving someone directions to your house, you might visualize the landmarks as you imagine driving from the starting point to your home.

Or, if you want to remember word definitions, you could visualize a picture of the definition in your mind. Look at the word "insuperable" which means "unable to overcome." To remember the definition you could visualize a soup can thinking about jumping over a wall. Or, if you want to remember the definition of the word "inclination," you could picture an image of the United States leaning (inclined nation).

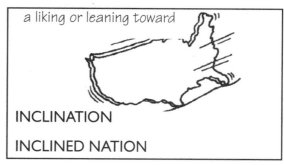

Practice Activity: Creating Visual Images to Improve Memory of Vocabulary Words

List three examples of how you have used visual images to improve your memory of some facts.

1. _____

2. _____

3. _____

Strategy: Using Association to Improve Memory

We can learn new information more easily when we associate it with something we are already familiar with, such as a picture, phrase, a story, a song, or a rhyme. See some examples below.

Memorizing by Using Association

Example:

To learn capitals of U.S. states:	**Use:**
Juneau, Alaska	Too cold to go to **Alaska** except in **June**.
Hartford, Connecticut	**Connected hearts**
Springfield, Illinois	You can't **spring** out of bed if you're **ill**.
Baton Rouge, Louisiana	**Louis** puts **rouge on** with a **bat**.
Augusta, Maine	It's **mainly** hot in **August**.
Helena, Montana	**Helen** climbs a **mountain**.
Columbus, Ohio	**Columbus** said, "**Oh, Hi!**"
Tallahassee, Florida	**Tall Floridian**

Practice Activity: Using Association to Improve Memory

Directions: Create associations for facts you are learning in one of your classes in school.

Facts   Association

_____   _____

_____   _____

_____   _____

_____   _____

Strategy: Improving Recall by Practicing Memorization

Memorization requires repetition. A musician learning to play a new song needs to practice over and over to master the piece. A basketball player improves his/her ability to make a three-point shot by practicing so his/her "muscle memory" becomes automatic.

If you wanted to learn a list of words, you can have someone recite the list to you several times so that each time you hear the list your ability to recall words would improve. If you wanted to remember facts in your text book, reading the facts several times and trying to remember them each time will no doubt improve your memory.

So then it makes sense that any of the memory methods we just covered will work best when you practice. This is a key point to improve recall and memory. Another key point is that you should frequently test yourself to see how well your memory is working. Practice until your memory is perfect.

In addition, we all have preferred learning styles. Some people remember things they hear (auditory learner), some remember things they see (visual learner), and some remember best by doing (kinesthetic learners).

If you are an **auditory learner,** since you remember better what you hear, rehearse by:

- repeating the information to be memorized out loud
- recording what you've said to listen later

If you are an **visual learner,** since you remember better what you see, rehearse by:

- reading the information
- visualizing associations
- drawing pictures

If you are an **kinesthetic learner**, since you remember better what you can do, rehearse by:

- jotting down brief notes
- outlining, mind-mapping or taking combo notes
- drawing pictures
- using objects that represent information

If you are a **combination learner**, since you remember better when you use more than one method, rehearse by:

- choosing a combination of strategies that would work well for the type of content you need to memorize

Practice Activity: Test How Well You Can Remember a Large Set of Facts

Now we're going to test you to see how well you can apply one or more of the memory strategies described earlier. Below is information about the first 10 U.S. presidents. Over the next few days study these facts by any means you like. Then answer the questions that follow to see how many facts about each president you have been able to recall.

Facts about the first 10 U.S. presidents

1. George Washington

   - only president elected unanimously

   - gave the shortest inauguration speech on record (133 words and less than two minutes long)

   - didn't have enough money to get to his inauguration—had to borrow $600 from a neighbor

   - at his inauguration, he had only one tooth left in his mouth

   - his false teeth were made from elephant and walrus tusks, not wood

2. John Adams

   - First president to live in the White House

   - in the election of 1796, Thomas Jefferson came in second to Adams by only three votes. Therefore, Adams served as president and Jefferson as vice-president for four years. This is the only time in American history that political opponents from different parties served as president and vice president

   - Adams and Jefferson were the only presidents to sign the Declaration of Independence

   - both Adams and Jefferson died on the same day—July 4th, on the 50th anniversary of the Declaration of Independence.

   - only one of two presidents whose son was also elected president

   - supported urban big business and national banking

3. Thomas Jefferson

   - spoke six different languages

   - First president to shake hands with guests — previously people bowed to presidents

   - First president to be inaugurated in Washington, D.C.

   - Jefferson supported farming and small business and opposed a national bank

   - had a family of plants named after him

4. James Madison

   - smallest president—5'4" and less than 100 pounds

   - only one of two presidents to sign U.S. Constitution (the other was Washington)

   - Nicknamed "Father of the Constitution"

   - British set fire to the White House while he was in office

---

5. James Monroe

 ■ third president to die on July 4th

 ■ First U.S. senator to become president

 ■ only president who didn't represent a political party

6. John Quincy Adams

 ■ First elected president who did not receive either the most electoral college votes or popular votes

 ■ elected by the House of Representatives because neither he or his opponent, Andrew Jackson, had enough electoral votes

 ■ only president elected to the House of Representatives after his presidency

 ■ First president to be photographed

7. Andrew Jackson

 ■ only president of a debt free U.S.

 ■ had no formal education

 ■ only president to have been a prisoner of war

 ■ only president to kill a man in a dual

 ■ First president to ride a railroad train

8. Martin Van Buren

 ■ First president born an American citizen

 ■ known as "Old Kinderhook" because he was raised in Kinderhook, N.Y. "OK" Clubs were created to support his campaign. Now "OK" is commonly used.

9. William Henry Harrison

 ■ holds the record for the longest inauguration speech (8578 words and one hour, 40 minutes long)

 ■ died of pneumonia after 31 days in office—most likely contracted while giving his inaugural speech

 ■ only president who studied to be a doctor

10. John Tyler

 ■ First vice-president to become president after a president's death

 ■ had 15 children—more than any other president

 ■ First president to have a veto overridden

1. Which strategies did you use to learn the information?

_____

_____

_____

_____

2. Which strategies were the most successful for you? Why?

_____

_____

_____

_____

3. Approximately how long did you study? (total time and over how many days?)

_____

_____

_____

_____

4. If you had to take a test on this material, do you think you would remember the information? Why or why not?

_____

_____

_____

_____

5. If the test is scheduled for two weeks from now, what can you do to retain the information?

_____

_____

_____

_____

6. Without looking back your notes, list as many facts as you can remember about these presidents.

1. George Washington _____

_____

2. John Adams _____

_____

3. Thomas Jefferson _____

_____

4. James Madison _____

_____

5. James Monroe _____

_____

6. John Quincy Adams _____

_____

7. Andrew Jackson _____

_____

8. Martin Van Buren _____

_____

9. William Henry Harrison _____

_____

10. John Tyler _____

_____

⊃ **Now ask yourself:**

How will my life be better now that I know how to improve my memory?

1.	
2.	

Teachers and Study Coaches: What can you do?

Before your presentation, plan to:

- ■ Minimize details so as not to overload students' memories.

- ■ Include advance organizers to activate students' prior knowledge.

- ■ Combine visual and verbal presentations.

- ■ Use concept maps, diagrams and webbing to increase visual input.

During your presentation:

- ■ Remind students to attend to what is important in your lectures and discussions.

- ■ Begin lectures with a "hook" to grab students' attention.

- ■ Emphasize important concepts by changing the pitch and pace of your speaking.

- ■ Rephrase, rather than repeat, important points.

- ■ Ask questions that require critical thinking, application and recall.

After your presentation:

- ■ Allow students access to your notes if they have significant learning issues with note taking and retaining information.

- ■ Allow students time to reflect and discuss what you've taught.

- ■ Assign students (in cooperative groups) the opportunity to create games, plays, songs or rhymes to aid retention of the information presented in your lesson.

- ■ Set up debates for students to question or try to disprove points.

- ■ Give frequent quizzes that allow you and your students to monitor their learning.

- ■ Assign homework that reinforces the most important concepts; grade effort and use mistakes for further teaching.

- ■ Add one or two details to current homework assignments that are from previous lessons, but will need to be recalled on future tests.

- ■ Review previously taught concepts at later times if they will need to be recalled for future tests.

Chapter Thirteen

TEST TAKING

*"If you do what you have always done,
you will get what you have always got."*

—Mark Twain

These are the skills that will be covered in this chapter.

Following directions
Developing effective study habits
Scoring high on all types of tests
Analyzing and using old tests
Efficient planning for mid-terms and finals

Sam hates taking tests. He feels his anxiety increase the minute he hears there's going to be one. Sometimes his teachers don't review or give out study sheets until the day before the test. Then Sam's up past midnight trying to cram in all that information the night before the test. How can his teachers expect anyone to remember so much in so little time?

Ali does okay on tests. She doesn't mind multiple choice tests, but never knows what she's supposed to do on those essays. Interestingly, her best friend Andy would rather have an all-essay test if only she could skip those multiple choice, true/false and matching parts.

You know what we're going to say about Sam. Of course he's nervous about and hates taking tests. He crams! This is not a good test taking strategy. As for Ali and Andy, they just need to learn how each part of a test works and how to approach it.

What is test taking?

Test taking allows teachers to evaluate how well students understand and are able to apply concepts and details from lessons. Tests are valuable to you because they let you see if you've understood what has been taught. They're also meaningful to your teachers because they allow teachers to evaluate how well they've explained the material. In this section, you will learn strategies that you will be able to apply to any exams, whether they are unit tests, finals, or standardized tests such as the SAT or ACT. You will learn how to be successful test-takers with less stress and better grades.

Survey: How Effective Are My Study Habits?

Complete this survey to determine the efficiency of your current study habits.

Directions: Think of a recent test you took in one of your content area classes (e.g., science, history, etc.) and fill out the following survey.

1. Before the test, I felt	_____ nervous _____ relaxed and confident
2. During the test, I felt	_____ confident that I knew and remembered the material _____ that I didn't know or couldn't recall the material well
3. The question types that were more difficult for me were the	_____ multiple choice _____ matching _____ true/false _____ fill-ins _____ essays
4. When I got my test grade, it was	_____ as I expected _____ lower than I expected _____ higher than I expected
5. The strategies that I used and seemed to help most were	_____ _____ _____
6. To better prepare for the next test, I will	_____ _____ _____

Practice Activity: Today's Test

Before you begin to learn the strategies in this chapter, take the following test. You have three minutes to complete it.

Name _____ Date _____

Directions:

1. Read all directions before your begin.

2. Write the city and state where you live.

3. Cross out all vowels.

4. Count the number of letters that remain.

5. Multiply that number by your age.

6. Divide by your grade. Round off to the nearest whole number.

7. Add the numbers of hours in a day.

8. Subtract the number of letters in your first and last names.

9. Divide by two.

10. Directions two through nine do not need to be done.

Work Space:

Strategy: Read All Test Directions

Read all directions carefully before you begin!

If you did no work on "Today's Test" then either you've seen it before or you already know to read the directions first. If you did some or all of the work before you realized the trick, you now know that you always need to read directions first.

Strategy: Taking Tests

Read this list of strategies for preparing for, monitoring, and assessing tests. The list of strategies for before taking tests is a review of what you learned in previous chapters of *Study Strategies Plus*. The list of strategies under *during* and *after* are those presented in this and subsequent chapters.

Before:

■ **Be prepared.** In the previous chapters, you learned how to be an active reader, take accurate notes, and efficiently learn the information relevant for tests.
If there are any that you are not following, go back to those chapters for a refresher and then include them in your daily study routine.

If you are consistently following those strategies you:

- pay attention in class

- listen to teachers' lectures for test cues

- do your homework in a thoughtful way

- actively read

- take good notes

- make study sheets

- review your notes within 24 hours and on a regular basis

- practice retrieval

- decide which memorization techniques will work best for type of information to be on the test

- attend review sessions

- estimate how long you need to study, starting well before the test date

- schedule study sessions well before the test date so you don't cram and are rested the night before the test

- determine how, when and with whom to study using your preferred learning styles

- write main ideas and important details on flash cards to do a quick review before the test

- have all supplies you need available and accessible

During:

■ **Monitor.** While you are taking tests, there are specific strategies you can utilize to monitor your progress. When you do this, you will have a more successful outcome.

If you consistently follow these strategies you:

- note the beginning and end time you have to complete the test, then pace yourself.

- take a quick look at the entire test for an overview (if it's allowed).

- practice relaxation techniques, such as deep breathing.

- read all directions carefully and ask for help if you don't understand something.

- write any mnemonic or outline that will trigger your recall of facts.

- do the easiest first.

- learn the strategies in this section for each type of test (multiple choice, matching, fill-ins, short answers and essays).

- check the clock. If you're running out of time, complete questions that are worth more points than others or are the ones you are more confident about.

After:

■ **Evaluate.** After you finish taking a test, you aren't done. There are still strategies you should use that will allow you to better prepare for any upcoming tests.

If you consistently follow these strategies you:

- jot down questions you were unsure of so you can check the answer when you get home.

- think of how well you followed the strategies you learned. While the test is fresh in your mind, write down any changes that you'll need to make before the next test.

- use any review your teacher has to evaluate why you missed answers and plan for the next test.

- meet with a teacher who does not review in class to evaluate any test on which you received a disappointing grade.

Two Categories of Tests: Objective and Subjective

1. Objective Tests

Objective tests are given more often than subjective tests. They have a right or wrong answer that is backed up by facts.

The four objective tests are:

- matching
- fill-ins
- true/false
- multiple choice

Six General Rules for Taking Objective Tests:

1. Read all of the directions.

2. Determine how many questions are on the test and how much time you will have.

3. Estimate how much time you will be able to spend on each question.

4. Answer the easiest first then complete the more difficult ones.

5. Guess by using process of elimination unless you are penalized for wrong answers.

6. If you are taking a Scantron test, keep checking that you are bubbling in the answers in the right places.

Preparing for Matching Tests

Matching tests usually require you to match words or phrases in one column with related phrases in another.

Matching is often used to test:

- vocabulary
- people and what they're known for
- historical events
- scientific occurrences

Three Strategies Specific to Matching Tests:

1. Count all the choices in each column. Start on the column that contains fewer choices that way you won't be bothered with the "ringer," which is the one that has no match.

2. If both columns have the same number of choices, start with the explanations that could contain clues.

3. As you choose an answer, lightly cross it out so you don't read it again.

Practice Activity: U.S. Presidents Matching Test

Directions: Put the letter of each description next to the president's name.

_____ 1. Barak Obama	_____ 5. Harry S. Truman
_____ 2. George W. Bush	_____ 6. Richard Nixon
_____ 3. Franklin Delano Roosevelt	_____ 7. Bill Clinton
_____ 4. John F. Kennedy	_____ 8. Ronald Reagan

A. This 43rd president was the son of the 41st president.

B. This president was a peanut farmer from Georgia.

C. This president said "Ask not what your country can do for you, ask what you can do for your country."

D. This president's wife became a senator and secretary of state.

E. This president was the first African-American elected to the presidency.

F. This president told the USSR to "tear down that wall" [dividing Berlin, Germany].

G. This president resigned in disgrace.

H. This president was the only one who was elected to a third and fourth term.

Preparing for Fill-Ins

Fill-in-the-blank questions are complete statements with a key word or phrase missing. Correct answers make the statement true. Answers to this type of question are often main ideas or supporting details.

Three Strategies Specific to Fill-in-the-Blank Tests:

1. If you know the answer, write it in, then read it to make sure it makes sense.

2. If you are unsure of the answer, leave it blank, but make a mark beside it to remind you to come back to it. You may find clues to its answer in another question.

3. If there is a word bank, cross out the words you have used.

Practice Activity: Fill-in Questions

Directions: Read each statement and write the appropriate word on the blank line.

1. An _____ triangle has all three sides of equal length. The angles all measure 60 degrees.

2. Obtuse angles measure greater than _____ and less than _____ degrees.

3. The formula for the area of a triangle is _____.

4. This four-sided polygon that has exactly one pair of parallel sides is called a _____.

5. An eight-sided polygon whose sum of angles is 1080 degrees is a _____.

6. The distance around a circle is called the _____.

7. _____ lines have two lines in the same plane that never intersect.

8. Two lines _____ when they share a common point.

9. Two lines that meet at a right angle are _____.

10. An _____ is a triangle having two sides of equal length.

Answers can be found in the Appendix.

Preparing for True/False Tests

True/false tests are statements that are either totally true or totally false.

Three Strategies Specific to True/False Tests:

1. Pay attention to the clues and key words.
   - ▪ Absolutes are "all" or "nothing" word clues. They *often* signal that the statement is false because few things happen "always" or "never."

ALL	ONLY
ALWAYS	NONE
EVERY	NEVER

   - ▪ These are words that usually signal true statements.

SOME	MAINLY
USUALLY	OFTEN
SELDOM	EXCEPT
SOMETIMES	RARELY
PROBABLY	

2. Pay attention to the sequence in statements.
   - ▪ Even if the facts are accurate, if the sequence is wrong, the statement is false.

     Example: The president following Richard Nixon was John F. Kennedy.

     Accurate facts: Nixon and Kennedy were presidents.

3. Pay attention to the entire statement.
   - ▪ If any part is false, the entire statement is false.

Practice Activity: True/False Test

Directions: The following statements include information from some of the academic subjects you study in school, so you should be familiar with most of the content. Read the sentences and if the statement is true, write **T** on the line. If the statement is false, write **F** on the line.

1. _____ All musicians can read music.

2. _____ It seldom snows in tropical climates.

3. _____ George Washington was elected president after Abraham Lincoln.

4. _____ There is only one meaning for the word "play."

5. _____ In the United States, presidential elections are held every six years.

6. _____ Verbs include action words such as run, play, sing, dance.

7. _____ Computers can always out-think people.

8. _____ Studying never helps improve grades.

9. _____ Most teachers are right-handed.

10. _____ Algebra is the study of angles, planes and two and three dimensional figures.

Answers can be found in the Appendix.

Preparing for Multiple Choice Tests

Multiple choice is the most frequently used format for testing. The questions often focus on details, so they should be in your notes and recall questions. They can seem difficult because more than one answer seems right, and two may be similar, so you have to decide which one is the best choice.

Five Strategies Specific to Multiple Choice Tests:

1. Read the question and identify the main idea. Then try to predict an answer before reading the choices.

2. Read all the answer choices and eliminate (cross out) any you know are wrong.

3. Choose the answer that makes the most sense to you based on the topics and details you have studied. Its subject should match the main idea of the question.

4. If two answers are too close, don't choose either one, but if two choices are almost opposite, choose one of them.

5. For negative questions ("which one is NOT a reason…" or "the author mentioned everything EXCEPT…"), think of what was included in what you have read, and eliminate those choices. If you are correct, you should only be left with one answer.

Practice Activity: Multiple Choice Test

Directions: Circle the letter of the answer that best completes each statement.

1. The capital of the United States is:
   a. London, England
   b. Butte, Montana
   c. Austin, Texas
   d. Washington, D.C.
   e. New York, New York

2. The national anthem of the U.S. is:
   a. The Star Spangled Banner
   b. American Pie
   c. America the Beautiful
   d. Glory, Glory, Hallelujah
   e. This Land is My Land, This Land is Your Land

3. The head of the British monarchy is:
   a. the president
   b. the prime minister
   c. the king or queen
   d. the Beatles
   e. none of the above

4. The part of the sentence that tells who or what the sentence is about is the:
   a. direct object
   b. verb
   c. subject
   d. predicate
   e. noun

Answers can be found in the Appendix.

5. The clause that describes a noun or pronoun is:
   a. Santa
   b. adverb
   c. independent
   d. adjective
   e. subordinate

6. Vertebrates all:
   a. have back bones and spinal columns
   b. have no back bones or spinal columns
   c. can swim
   d. lay eggs
   e. walk erect on two legs

7. Luna, the Earth's moon has:
   a. beaches
   b. its own source of light and heat
   c. mountains, valleys, old volcano sites and craters
   d. never been walked on by humans
   e. stopped orbiting the Earth

8. When adding positive and negative numbers, remember that:
   a. two negatives equal a positive
   b. two positives equal a negative
   c. a negative plus a positive equals a positive
   d. a positive plus a negative equals a positive
   e. none of the above

9. To solve a math problem, the order of operations is done:
   a. in any order
   b. from left to right
   c. from right to left
   d. from the inside out
   e. none of the above

10. All of the following are states EXCEPT:
    a. Oregon
    b. Nebraska
    c. Washington, D.C.
    d. Minnesota
    e. New Mexico

Practice Activity: Recall What You've Learned About Objective Tests

I. Read the following statements and circle the letter of the best answer.

1. Facts and details are tested.
   a. matching   b. fill-ins   c. true/false   d. multiple choice   e. all of the above

2. This type of test often contains absolutes like "all" or "never."
   a. matching   b. fill-ins   c. true/false   d. multiple choice   e. all of the above

3. Answer the easier questions first.
   a. matching   b. fill-ins   c. true/false   d. multiple choice   e. all of the above

4. Start with the column that has fewer choices.
   a. matching   b. fill-ins   c. true/false   d. multiple choice   e. all of the above

5. Try to predict an answer before reading the choices.
   a. matching   b. fill-ins   c. true/false   d. multiple choice   e. all of the above

Answers can be found in the Appendix.

II. Read the statement and fill in the answer that best completes it.

6. The first step when taking a test is to _____.

7. In order for a statement to be true, the _____ must be true.

8. Writing and reviewing _____ is helpful when taking objective tests.

9. There are _____ types of objective tests.

10. If you are unsure of an answer, _____ unless you are penalized for wrong answers.

III. Write (T) if the answer is true and (F) if it is false.

11. _____ For matching tests, if both columns have an equal number of choices, begin with the explanations first.

12. _____ Words such as "some," "usually," and "probably" are always found in true statements.

13. _____ The order of information can determine whether the statement is true or false.

14. _____ Multiple choice questions can be tricky because choices may seem similar.

15. _____ Always guess on fill-in tests.

IV Match the word in column A with its explanation in column B.

2. Subjective Tests

Subjective tests are usually essays. Unlike objective tests, information can include opinions. Carefully follow directions and teacher requirements. You will also want to make sure that your ideas are supported by what you've read and what is included in teachers' lessons and lectures.

A	B
_____ 16. ringer	a. answers may be opinions
_____ 17. objective	b. the extraneous choice on a matching test
_____ 18. subjective	c. often signals false on a true/false test
_____ 19. never	d. type of test given most often in school
_____ 20. Scantron	e. a separate answer sheet that requires you to "bubble" in answers
	f. read these before starting on the test

Preparing for Essay Tests

Writing an essay is your chance to demonstrate not only what you know about the topic, but how you can support your ideas with facts. If you are also asked to give your opinion, keep it brief and include evidence to show you're right.

Know these key words that are often part of essay questions or directions. These words require you to write all the *relevant* information you know about the topic:

- Describe
- Discuss
- Explain

- List
- Outline
- Prove

- Review
- State

These words signal you to write facts in a specific way:

- Compare — Write the similarities and differences about the subject.
- Contrast — Write about the differences only.
- Compare and Contrast — Write about the similarities and differences of the subjects.
- Define — Write the meaning of the word or subject.
- Illustrate — Write examples that would paint a picture about the topic.
- Diagram — Draw and carefully label charts, tables, time lines, etc.

These words require you to write your opinion and support it with facts:

- Criticize
- Evaluate

- Interpret
- Justify

Twelve Strategies Specific to Essay Tests:

Before:

1. Know how many essays you are asked to write and the time you'll have for each.

2. Begin with the essay easiest for you.

3. Underline any key words that are in the question, such as compare, interpret, etc.

4. Write your ideas in the margin and then number them in the order you want to use them, beginning with your strongest idea (think of this as your rough outline).

During:

5. Begin by restating the prompt or question

   - Find the subject of the prompt or question
   - Turn it into your thesis sentence which will mention the topic, your position, and one to three reasons why you believe what you do. These will be your controlling ideas. They will also be your organizational guide.

6. Make your details specific (the day before the test, refer back to your notes and recall questions).

7. Include vocabulary from your notes in your essay.

8. Skip lines between paragraphs so you have room to add when you edit.

9. Write legibly; you will lose unnecessary points if the teacher can't read your writing.

10. Be concise and well organized.

After:

11. Reread. Did you answer the question? Did you answer all the questions? Even if you can only write a little, partial credit is better than no credit.

12. Proofread for grammar, punctuation or spelling errors and NEATNESS.
(It's always frustrating to write a good essay, then lose points due to faulty grammar, spelling or sloppy handwriting.) If handwriting is truly an issue for you, ask if you are eligible for accommodations such as using a computer.

Practice Activity: Turning the Essay Prompt or Question Into Your Lead Sentence

Read the essay question prompts below and restate them as lead sentences. You don't need to know anything about the topic; just look for the subject and rewrite it. In some, you may want to include the stand you would take (whether you agree or disagree). We have done the first one for you.

Example:

The question:	Discuss the benefits or liabilities of requiring all students to wear school uniforms.
Your sentence:	Requiring all students to wear uniforms allows students to focus less on what they wear and more on what they need to learn.

[Notice that in the example, the subject was the requirement of uniforms. In the sentence, we restated that and gave an opinion.]

1. The question: Compare and contrast how students of the 20th century got information for research to the way you do.

Your sentence: _____

_____

2. The question: Do standardized tests, such as the SAT, really assess what students know and should colleges continue to use them?

Your sentence: _____

_____

3. The question: Explain the various theories, such as a meteorite, disease or climate change, as reasons why dinosaurs became extinct.

Your sentence: _____

_____

4. The question: Describe how the innovations of how we communicate and store information like music has affected your life and our culture as a whole.

Your sentence: _____

_____

Practice Activity: Discussing the Subject

Directions: Review the article and your highlighting about Henry VIII used in the **3-Sweep Strategy** section. Then use the information to discuss how Henry VIII managed to change the course of religion in England.

_____

_____

_____

_____

_____

_____

_____

_____

_____

_____

_____

_____

_____

_____

_____

_____

_____

_____

_____

Strategy: Preparing for Open-book or Open-note Tests

Sometimes you will be allowed to refer to your books and/or notes as you take an exam. Though it sounds like a "gimme," open book tests can be harder than other tests.

1. Thoroughly prepare for this test as if you couldn't have your books with you.

2. Be familiar with the location of the main points in the book.

3. Use sticky notes and tabs to "bookmark" important details to help you quickly find them.

4. If you can also have notes or index cards, briefly note down words to trigger your recall about the main points or details. That way you won't need to take the time to search through your book.

5. First answer questions that you know without referring to your book. It will save you time.

Practice Activity: Test—The First 10 U.S. Presidents

Your final activity in the Memory for Better Grades chapter was to use the strategies from that chapter to learn facts about the first ten presidents. Now you will take a test of the information.

I. Multiple choice: Read the following statements and circle the letter of the best answer choice. (4 points each)

1. When he was president, the United States had no debt.

    A. William Henry Harrison   C. Andrew Jackson

    B. Glover Cleveland   D. James Monroe

2. He was nicknamed "Father of the Constitution."

    A. Theodore Roosevelt   C. Martin Van Buren

    B. James Madison   D. John Tyler

3. He was elected president by the House of Representatives.

    A. John Adams   C. John Quincy Adams

    B. Zachary Taylor   D. James Madison

4. He was the first president to live in the White House.

    A. Andrew Johnson   C. Thomas Jefferson

    B. James Monroe   D. James Adams

5. He was the first vice-president to become president after a president's death.

    A. Lyndon Johnson   C. John Tyler

    B. James Madison   D. William Henry Harrison

Answers can be found in the Appendix.

II. Matching: Match the information in column A with the correct president in column B.
(4 points each)

A

____ 6. gave the longest presidential speech

____ 7. elected unanimously

____ 8. first president to be photographed

____ 9. first president who was an American citizen

___10. had no formal education

B

A. Martin Van Buren

B. John Quincy Adams

C. John Tyler

D. James Monroe

E. William Henry Harrison

F. George Washington

G. Andrew Jackson

III. Fill-in the blanks: Read the statement and fill the answer that best completes the
statement. (4 points each)

11. _____ was the only president elected to the House of Representatives
after being president.

12. The only two presidents to sign the U.S. Constitution were George Washington and
_____.

13. _____ was only one of two presidents to have his son elected as president.

14. _____ had the shortest time in office as president.

15. _____ had to borrow money to get to his own inauguration.

IV. True and False: Write (T) if the statement is true and (F) if the statement is false.
(4 points each)

16. ___ George Washington's false teeth were made of wood.

17. ___ The British set fire to the White House when James Monroe was president.

18. ___ John Quincy Adams was the first president who did not receive either the most
electoral college votes or popular votes.

19. ___ John Tyler was the third president to die on July 4th.

20. ___ Thomas Jefferson spoke six different languages.

V. Essay: Compare and contrast the lives and presidencies of John Adams and Thomas Jefferson.
(10 points each). Use a separate page for this activity.

Strategy: Making Old Tests Work for You!

One of the most valuable study aids you have is a test you've already taken that is returned to you. By analyzing your errors, you can learn from your mistakes and actually plan ways to score higher on future tests. Also, if information was important enough to be included on a test, it may show up again on your mid-term or final exam. Sometimes teachers do not return tests or only review them briefly during class. In these cases, speak with your teacher to arrange a time to meet to review the test. Bring this book so you can fill in the following charts.

Practice Activity: Making Old Tests Work for You

Directions: For this activity, use a test that your teacher has returned to you. If one is not available, use the test you took in this section about the U.S. presidents. However, in that case, you will not be able to answer some of the questions in this activity. Leave those blank until you are able to use this strategy for actual tests you've taken in school.

1. Check the types of questions that were included on your test, then list the number of each type question you got wrong.

Question type	Number of questions included	Number of questions missed
Matching		
True/False		
Fill-In		
Multiple Choice		
Short Answer		
Essay		

Which types of questions did you miss the most? _____

Did you miss more objective _____ or subjective _____ questions?

⊃ *Review the test taking strategies for those types of questions you missed.*

2. Look at the first question you missed and find its answer in your textbook or notes. Then answer the following questions and fill out the chart with (Y) for Yes or (N) for no:

Question missed	Was it highlighted?	In your notes?	Had you written recall questions about it?

⮑ *For any (N) answers, go back to review the "3-Sweeps," "Note taking," and "Recall Questions" strategies and begin today to apply the strategies until you become proficient.*

3. For this test, did you cram the night before____? study over several days____? practice retrieval____? use specific memory techniques___?

4. Use what you've learned about how you studied for this test to better prepare for the next test.

Before the next test I plan to:

1. _____

2. _____

3. _____

4. _____

5. _____

⮑ *When you receive an old test, write down the correct answers for any questions you got wrong. You may see these questions again (perhaps worded differently) on mid-terms or finals. Be sure to save your vocabulary cards, notes, and graded tests, filing them by subject and chapter.*

Strategy: Preparing for Mid-term and Final Exams

Mid-term and final exams are administered to test your ability to organize, understand and recall what has been taught over a period of weeks or months. Your tests are often for more than one class, yet are all given at around the same time. No wonder you can feel overwhelmed.

However, since you have been following the strategies in *Study Strategies Plus*, you have been reading, doing homework, highlighting, writing recall questions and practicing retrieval of information for your classes over a long period of time. You should feel prepared when mid-terms and finals come around. You can take those tests with confidence.

Prepare at least two weeks before mid-terms or finals.

A. Find out all you can about the exam:

1. What will the test format be?

    a. For objective questions, focus on memorizing important details.

    b. For essays, focus on main ideas and their supporting details.

2. Will you be allowed to bring notes? In what format are their limitations?

3. Will any chapters, topics or materials not be included? If you don't know this, study everything!

4. Listen for teachers' clues.

5. Attend study sessions.

B. Start preparing

   1. Organize your filed notes and old tests.

   2. Make sure you highlighted and wrote recall questions; if you haven't try to do it now.

   3. Write your study schedule for the next two weeks on your calendar. Be realistic as to how many days you have and how much time you can devote to each subject.

C. Organize your study sessions

   1. Follow your study schedule and pace yourself so that you study a little each day.

   2. Divide the number of chapters to cover by the number of days you set aside for study.

   3. Study each subject for 20 - 30 minutes, then take a break before beginning the next subject (refer back to the 20+5 strategy).

   4. Study textbook chapters, their study questions and your associated notes and recall questions.

   5. Review old tests since similar questions and content will be on mid-term and final tests.

D. Use your stronger learning styles and preferences

   1. Refer back to the learning styles chapter of *Study Strategies Plus* to remind you of how and when you prefer to study.

   2. Plan to take advantage of your strengths.

E. Cramming

   1. DON'T.

   2. If you must cram, be efficient and concentrate on the highlighted notes and recall questions since it will be the most important and you may be able to store it into your memory in a short amount of time. Crammed information doesn't last very long!

F. Suggestions from successful test takers

   1. Successful test takers relax before exams because they know they've done all they could to prepare.

   2. They go to sleep early the night before an exam.

   3. They wake up early to eat a nutritious breakfast.

   4. They listen to soothing music (or music that makes them feel good).

   5. They believe they will do well and enter the exam room with confidence.

   6. Take advice from those who don't fear mid-terms and finals and become a successful test taker, too. You can do it!

⊃ **Now ask yourself:**

How will my life be better now that I know how to take different types of tests?

1.	
2.	

Teachers: What can you do?

Before a test:

- ■ Be clear about what you expect students to understand about the unit you are teaching.

- ■ Make sure that your homework assignments reinforce the important points of your lessons.

- ■ Be available for study sessions and provide constructive feedback after homework is returned.

- ■ Make sure that the tests reflect what students were expected to learn and that directions are clear.

During a test:

- ■ Make sure that the room is as distraction-free as possible.

- ■ Be ready to clarify directions if students have plausible questions about them.

After a test:

- ■ If at all possible, after you have graded a test and are reviewing it with your classes, give the questions and students' answers back to them. If you cannot allow them to take the tests home, you will really appreciate and your students will benefit from using the strategy, Making Old Tests Work for You.

- ■ By teaching your students to self-evaluate, you are teaching them to take responsibility for their grades and take steps to improve their study habits before the next test.

Chapter Fourteen

HANDLING HOMEWORK

❝I like a teacher who gives you something to take home to think about besides homework.❞

–Edith Ann, [Lily Tomlin]

These are the skills that will be covered in this chapter.

Using a planner or assignment book

Finding a good homework space where you can concentrate

Exerting thought and effort on assignments

Completing homework and turning it in on time

During the week, Anthony has baseball practices, music lessons and other after-school activities. When is he supposed to get his homework done, especially when there is so much homework to do and some that he didn't understand? His parents try to help, but Anthony thinks that they are always nagging him. When that happens, he feels frustrated and angry.

Anthony's parents would describe their evenings when Anthony has homework as a "battle zone." Should they push him to get it done? Should they help him? How much help should they give him? A lot? A little? None? They often wish teachers would not assign any homework.

Anthony's teachers described their concern about homework as one of their most troubling. Mrs. Perez, Anthony's science teacher said, "I assign homework to reinforce new concepts, and so that Anthony can check whether he understands. I want Anthony's parents to be involved, but I don't want them to do his homework for him. If Anthony's work is incorrect, I can help him."

Mr. Jackson, Anthony's English teacher: "Homework helps Anthony to learn. We teachers try to coordinate when and how much homework we assign, but sometimes that's difficult. Anthony needs to learn how to budget his time. I give homework because when Anthony goes to college and then starts his career, he'll need to have the skills he gets from doing homework."

Why must we do homework?

Practice Activity: Homework...Two Viewpoints

Everyone knows how much students dislike homework, so here's your chance to list your top five complaints about it. Be as clear and candid as you wish.

1. _____

2. _____

3. _____

4. _____

5. _____

Teachers feel differently about assigning homework. List five reasons that your teachers think assigning homework is beneficial.

1. _____

2. _____

3. _____

4. _____

5. _____

Students, though we feel your pain, research supports your teachers' ideas about the importance of homework when the right kind of assignments are given. Homework is designed to reinforce the concepts your teachers have introduced in class. It should be just enough for you to practice for understanding. You should be able to do it independently, though you may need your parents or study coach to clarify some points.

Here's the scoop from all that fancy research:

■ Research indicates students need to practice a skill up to 24 times until they reach 80% competency. Further, since schooling occupies only about 13% of the waking hours of the first 18 years of life, which is less time then kids spend watching television, it is important that students have opportunities to practice skills they learned at school at home so that they can master them.

■ At the secondary school level, student homework is associated with greater academic achievement. Specifically, at the high school level, for about every 30 minutes of "additional" homework a student does per night, his or her overall grade point average (GPA) increases about half a point. This means that if a student with a GPA of 2.00 increases the amount of homework she does by 30 minutes per night, her GPA could rise to 2.50. These results speak for themselves. An appropriate amount of homework, at the appropriate level with the purpose of practice, retention, extension, and enhancement can improve academic achievement.

Students: What can you do?

Practice Activity: How Do You Complete Homework Now?

Directions: Read the questions below and circle the letter that best describes your homework habits.

1. When homework is assigned, how do you usually remember what to do?

   a. I immediately write assignments including all directions in my planner (or put it in a computer, smart phone, etc.).

   b. I write it on a notebook page in that subject's folder.

   c. I write it down on any available paper.

   d. I don't write it or enter it anywhere; I just remember it.

2. Where do you usually do your homework?

   a. in my room

   b. in my family's kitchen or family room

   c. at a friend's house

   d. at school during my free or study hall time

3. When do you usually do your homework?

   a. right after I get home from school

   b. late in the evening, often just before I go to bed

   c. early in the morning before school

   d. in class

4. How much total time do you usually spend on homework per day (on average)?

   a. under a half hour

   b. about an hour

   c. my entire afternoon and night

   d. almost no time

5. Think of an assignment with a due date at least a week or month away. What do you usually do?

   a. I do it immediately to get it out of the way.

   b. I do a little of it each day.

   c. I procrastinate until a day or so before it's due, then scramble to get it done on time.

   d. I schedule when to work on it until it's done.

6. What is your attitude about homework?

   a. It's a waste of my time.

   b. I don't love it, but know it's a necessity.

   c. I don't mind doing it if I am learning from it.

   d. I actually enjoy doing homework.

7. Which subject's homework seem most helpful to your learning? Why?

   _____

8. Which subject's homework seem least helpful to your learning? Why?

   _____

9. Do you think you could do something to get more out of your homework?
   ____ Yes ____ No

10. Are you willing to use strategies you learn from *Study Strategies Plus* to change the way you do homework? ____ Yes ____ No

Practice Activity: Reinforce The Best Homework Practices

Directions: Use this check list below to make sure you are doing homework properly.

Before you start your homework:

☐ Make sure your workspace is clear.

☐ Be certain that you have all assignments listed in your planner or cell phone (make sure you have all the requirements, pages, etc.).

☐ Check that you have the books and materials needed to complete your assignments.

☐ Prioritize the order you plan to do your assignments and estimate how long each assignment will take to complete. (Review the Planning and Prioritizing chapter).

☐ Let your family and friends know that you'll need privacy (that means no phone calls or texting).

☐ Break each task into manageable chunks.

☐ Ask a friend or relative to check on your progress (both of you agree and write down how often and in what way that will happen).

While you are doing your homework:

☐ Keep the phone and TV off but if you need background noise, turn on music (please keep it a bit softer than you usually like it).

☐ Follow your plan for pacing yourself so that you are putting in full effort, taking a short break (no more than five minutes) after about 20 minutes of work.

☐ Place your work in the correct folder when you finish each assignment.

☐ Ask yourself:

– Do I understand the directions?

– Have I correctly done the first few examples?

– Am I using the study strategies I learned for this? Are they working or do I need to ask for help, re-read or put it aside?

– Am I on task? Can I finish this in the time I estimated?

After you have done your homework:

☐ Ask yourself:

– Did I follow all directions and include every part of the assignment?

– Do I feel as though I put in the effort I needed to earn the grade I want?

– Do I need to ask someone to check my work?

– Where will I put the completed work? (e.g., bookbag, folder?)

– Where will I put my (bookbag) so that I see it and remember to take it to school?

⊃ **Now ask yourself:**

How will my life be better now that I know strategies to handle homework?

1.	
2.	

Teachers and Study Coaches: What can you do?

■ Communicate your specific homework policy to students and parents:

- Your purpose for assigning homework

- The average amount of time assignments should take students

- Where you post assignments (on board, website, etc.) and how students and parents can access it

- Consequences for missed or late homework

- How parents can be involved

■ Research shows that homework is more effective if followed by specific feedback, so try to be timely and consistent with specific, constructive feedback to students and when appropriate, to parents.

■ Set up a homework blog that allows students to work cooperatively.

■ If possible, help students on a 504 plan or IEP to acquire a second set of books.

■ Make your homework assignments count by focusing on depth of understanding rather than quantity.

■ For students with processing speed deficits, reduce the amount of assignments with just enough for students to demonstrate mastery.

Chapter Fifteen

STRESS MANAGEMENT

"My motto was always to keep swinging.
Whether I was in a slump or feeling badly or having
trouble off the field, the only thing to do was keep swinging."
—Hank Aaron

These are the skills that will be covered in this chapter.

> Believing in yourself
>
> Staying calm about school work
>
> Reducing stress by relaxing

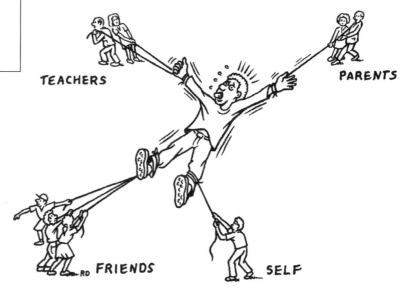

What is stress management?

Every person experiences stress at some points and to various degrees. As students, you sometimes feel stressed by teachers, parents, school work and tests, as well as from friends. Some of you also may make demands upon yourselves, which causes you stress.

The way we react emotionally to these stressors can affect our performance in school. Athletes know that to perform at their best, they need to be in top shape, both mentally and physically. Most use psychological strategies to help them mentally prepare for the stresses they feel.

We have included a few of these sports psychology strategies in *Study Strategies Plus* to help you keep in top mental shape while performing in school.

Students: What can you do?

Practice Activity: Purposeful Positiveness

Looking at a glass that is half-filled with water, optimists are said to see it as half full, while pessimists see the glass as half empty. How you look at your life will affect your chances of success in school (and life). Positive thinkers face new challenges and obstacles with energy and confidence. They spend less time than negative thinkers do complaining about assignments, teachers and tests, or how they will get things done or fearing grades. Therefore, they have lots of mental energy available to be creative and productive.

Directions: Check either "yes" or "no" to answer these questions about yourself to see if you are a positive or negative thinker.

Yes   No

_____ _____ 1. I often enter a test situation thinking I am going to do well.

_____ _____ 2. I usually start a new assignment right away.

_____ _____ 3. When I write reports, I usually like the way they turn out.

_____ _____ 4. I am pretty optimistic about my grades on tests and papers.

_____ _____ 5. I usually feel good about myself and other people in my life.

If you answered "No" to most of these questions, you can probably use a good dose of positive thinking. Here's how you can begin to purposely change you negative thoughts into positive ones.

■ **Recognize the negative thoughts you have.** We sometimes get so used to thinking one way, that we don't recognize how negative our thinking is. On the next page, keep a diary for two days of all the negative thoughts you have. Thoughts such as, "Oh my gosh, I'm going to fail this test" or "I'll never be able to learn this math" or "I look awful today," count as negative thoughts.

■ **Use your list of negative thoughts and write the opposite, positive thought.** Repeat the positive thought aloud five times and then say it to yourself five times more.

■ **Practice thinking positive.** Once you've figured out what negative thoughts trouble you the most, turn them into positive thoughts. For many people, negative thinking has become a habit. Habits get stronger when we repeat them over and over. They get weaker when we do them less often or stop them altogether. By catching ourselves thinking negatively, replacing negative thoughts with positive ones, and repeating those positive thoughts over and over, we can replace a negative thinking habit with a positive thinking habit.

■ **Change your thoughts to positive ones.** If you find yourself dwelling on negative thoughts too much, stop thinking and change your thoughts to something else. This is like changing a radio station if you didn't like the song. Remember, you have control of how you think. Negative thinking never does anyone any good, while positive thinking does wonders. You'll feel better, and you'll perform better.

Practice Activity: Reverse—Don't Rehearse—Negative Thinking

Directions: Keep a diary of your thoughts for the next two days. Write down any negative thoughts that come to mind, then write down a positive thought to replace it.

NEG _____

POS _____

NEG _____

POS _____

NEG _____

POS _____

NEG _____

POS _____

NEG _____

POS _____

Remember, negative thinking is like a bad habit. The more you do it, the stronger the habit becomes. Reverse—don't rehearse—negative thinking. Recite the positive thoughts you've written to yourself and use them to replace negative thoughts in the future.

Practice Activity: Stay relaxed under stress

When faced with a stressor, our body's autonomic nervous system kicks into action. Our heart races and sends more blood to our muscles, brain, and organ systems to make them better prepared to deal with the stress. We become ready to protect ourselves from the stressor, either by fight or flight. Stress can lead to good things. For instance, stress over grades motivates us to study and be prepared. However, stress can also be damaging. Excessive stress can create physical problems, can interfere with our ability to concentrate or to sleep well at night, and can cause us to be moody or irritable.

Directions: Do you have any of the following stress indicators? Check the ones you get when you feel tense.

_____ headaches	_____ nervousness	_____ overly sensitive
_____ stomach aches	_____ restlessness	_____ change in appetite
_____ muscle tension	_____ irritable moods	_____ poor concentration
_____ difficulty sleeping	_____ excessive worrying	_____ angry outbursts

When stress gets out of hand and you begin to show signs of physical, social or emotional difficulties, you will need to learn to cope with it another way. Here are some ways that people have found to cope with stress:

- Work out. Get some physical exercise. Walking, jogging, swimming, yoga, etc. can take your mind of a problem and help your body recharge.

- Tell somebody how you feel. Talking about your feelings with someone you trust and will be supportive and understanding can help you feel better.

- Take a break from the pressure. If you feel overwhelmed by too much schoolwork, take time off. Look at your schedule to see if you can make any changes that would make your life easier.

- Analyze your thinking. Are you creating stress by thinking negatively? Are you being realistic? Look back at the Purposeful Positiveness activity to help you start to change negative thoughts into positive ones.

Strategy: Use Visualization to Relax

Visualization is an excellent strategy to help you achieve relaxation. By visualizing ourselves in a restful, relaxing environment, we can remove negative thoughts from our minds and experience a calm feeling throughout our bodies. This activity will help you focus on a scene which many people find relaxing. To do this, find a comfortable, quiet place that is free of distractions.

Imagine yourself taking a walk in a beautiful valley surrounded by mountains. You stop to relax on a grassy area near a stream. You find the perfect spot to rest and you lie down and close your eyes. Imagine yourself lying there—calm, peaceful, and relaxed. Your breathing becomes easy, your body begins to feel calm and your mind becomes quiet. You can hear the sound of birds chirping in the distance and the water running across the rocks in the stream. You can smell the fresh scent of the grass and flowers and feel the gentle breezes of the air around you. The sun warms your body and you feel quiet and relaxed.

As you lie there, repeat these three phrases to yourself:

I feel calm and relaxed.

My mind is at ease.

My body is relaxed.

Continue with this exercise for 10 minutes, occasionally repeating the phrases and visualizing the comforting scene.

Other relaxing visualizations can be floating in a pool, lying on the beach, lying in bed at home, sitting on a golf course or any place that makes you feel good.

Reducing Test Taking Anxiety

Most people feel nervous before tests. A little nervousness is okay and even helpful. However, if your worrying and nervousness interfere with your concentration, you may have test anxiety.

Some causes of test anxiety may be a lack of confidence, over-concern about grades and achievement, pressure from others, or failure to do well on tests in the past. If on the day of a test, your palms sweat, your nerves get rattled and your stomach does flip...you may be suffering from test anxiety.

Here's the good news! Test anxiety can be decreased. Do the activity on the next page to help you relax in a test situation.

Practice Activity: Desensitize Yourself to Test Anxiety

Directions: You can learn to become more relaxed before or during a test by using a process psychologists call systematic desensitization. This is really a simple process in which you relax while visualizing different test-taking scenes which cause nervousness.

Look at the list of test-taking scenarios that sometimes make students nervous:

1. thinking the night before about tomorrow's test.
2. waking up the morning of the test and thinking about it.
3. walking to school on the day of the test.
4. going into the classroom where you will take the test.
5. sitting at your desk with the test in front of you.
6. reading the test at your desk and answering the questions.

While you imagine each of the scenarios listed above, use the relaxation technique you learned in the previous section.

⊃ Now ask yourself:

How will my life be better now that I can manage stress?

1.	
2.	

Chapter Sixteen

CONCLUSION

A QUESTIONNAIRE OF EXECUTIVE FUNCTIONING AND STUDY STRATEGIES

You will learn new and more efficient ways of studying using *Study Strategies Plus*. Before you begin, take a few minutes to evaluate your present skills.

Directions: Read each question below. If you almost always do what is asked, write "Y." If you almost never do what is asked, write "N." If you sometimes do what is asked, though not enough, write "S." Then add up all of your "Y" responses and write the total number of those to get your Study Skills Rating.

ORGANIZATION

_____ 1. Do I have a neat, organized place to do my homework?

_____ 2. Do I have good organizing habits and organize regularly?

_____ 3. Do I keep my notebooks and materials organized so I can easily find what I need?

_____ 4. Do I frequently keep track of my grades?

TIME MANAGEMENT

_____ 5. Do I have a good sense of time so that I can estimate how long an assignment should take me?

_____ 6. Do I write down a time schedule of homework, study, and activities?

_____ 7. Do I budget my time so that I get everything done within required time limits?

_____ 8. Do I assess how my time budget went and plan changes if necessary?

STARTING, FOCUSING, AND FINISHING

_____ 9. Do I start assignments on my own without procrastinating?

_____ 10. Do I stick with assignments until they are completed?

_____ 11. Do I delay what is fun to work on an assignment that is required?

_____ 12. Do I complete and turn in my assignments on time?

PLANNING AND PRIORITIZING

_____ 13. Do I plan how to get my homework and studying done?

_____ 14. Do I follow a written action plan for getting work done?

_____ 15. Do I prioritize the work I need to do?

_____ 16. Do I make and follow a written plan to complete long-term assignments?

_____ 16. Do I make and follow a written plan to complete long-term assignments?

SELF-MONITORING AND METACOGNITION

_____ 17. Do I think about which learning style and strategies to use for a task?

_____ 18. Do I have a plan before starting an assignment?

_____ 19. Do I monitor how I'm doing and make changes if I need to?

_____ 20. Do I evaluate how I did and plan changes I might make for the next assignment?

LEARNING STYLES

_____ 21. Do I know my preferred learning styles?

_____ 22. Do I use my best styles of learning when I study?

_____ 23. Do I know in what environment I study best?

COMMUNICATION

_____ 24. Do I think that my teachers usually see my behaviors as positive?

_____ 25. Do I usually know what each teacher expects of me?

_____ 26. Do I know how to ask for help from teachers when I need it?

READING COMPREHENSION

_____ 27. Do I think about and pay attention to what I am reading?

_____ 28. Can I identify topics, main ideas, and supporting details in a reading selection?

_____ 29. Do I paraphrase what I read?

_____ 30. Do I use signal words to help me identify important information in my textbooks?

_____ 31. Do I preview textbook chapters?

_____ 32. Do I have successful methods to learn and retain new vocabulary?

SUMMARIZING AND NOTE TAKING

_____ 33. Do I summarize information from readings and lectures?

_____ 34. Do I know different ways to take notes?

_____ 35. Do I take accurate notes from lectures?

_____ 36. Do I use abbreviations for note taking?

_____ 37. Do I turn my notes into study sheets?

_____ 38. Do I consistently review my notes over a period of time?

MEMORY FOR BETTER GRADES

_____ 39. Do I understand how the three types of memory work for me?

_____ 40. Do I use a variety of techniques to memorize besides reading information over and over?

_____ 41. Do I use efficient ways to study and review for tests?

_____ 42. When I take tests, do I remember enough information to get the grades I want?

TEST TAKING

_____ 43. Do I begin studying from the first day a new unit is introduced?

_____ 44. While taking a test, do I carefully follow directions?

_____ 45. Do I know strategies for taking different kinds of tests?

_____ 46. Do I keep old tests and notes to use for mid-terms and finals?

_____ 47. Do I analyze my errors on tests to determine a pattern?

_____ 48. Do I effectively prepare for mid-terms and final exams?

_____ 49. Am I pleased with my current grades?

HANDLING HOMEWORK

_____ 50. Do I include all the directions of an assignment in my planner or cell phone?

_____ 51. Do I do homework in an environment that allows me to concentrate?

_____ 52. Do I exert enough thought and effort to get something meaningful out of my assignments?

_____ 53. Do I complete and turn in my homework by its due date?

STRESS MANAGEMENT

_____ 54. Am I confident that I can do well in school?

_____ 55. Do I usually feel calm and relaxed about school?

_____ 56. Do I know and use strategies to help me reduce stress?

WHAT IS YOUR STUDY SKILLS RATING?   SCORE: _____

50-56 Correct is 90% – 100% Superior

45-49 Correct is 80% – 89% Good

40-44 Correct is 70% – 79% Average

Less than 40 Correct is below 70% – Needs Improvement

Compare this score you received with the score you got before reading _Study Strategies Plus_. Do the Practice Activity on the following page, and you'll have a plan to refine your skills even more as you increase your school success!

Practice Activity: How is *Study Strategies Plus* working for you?

Directions: Now that you have learned the strategies in *Study Strategies Plus*, think about how they are beneficial and how you can utilize them to become an even better student.

1. List the strategies from *Study Strategies Plus* that you are consistently using.

_____

_____

_____

_____

2. Have you seen improvements in your grades?

_____ Yes

_____ No

If your answer is no, think about and discuss what you can do to improve your grades.

_____

_____

_____

_____

3. Are there additional goals you would like to achieve? List them and discuss your plan to reach them.

_____

_____

_____

_____

_____

_____

_____

_____

_____

_____

_____

APPENDIX

ANSWER KEY

READING COMPREHENSION

Page 77

Story 1:

Topic: *new laws*
Main Idea:
Did you find the main idea ___✔___ in the first sentences; _____ in the last sentences; _____ in the middle of the paragraph; _____ was unstated, had to be inferred.
Supporting detail: *Many auto accidents involve teenagers.*
Supporting detail: *Teenagers are not allowed to make calls or text while driving.*
Supporting detail: *Deaths and injuries due to phone calls and texting have dropped.*

Story 2:

Topic: *North Pole*
Main Idea: *The long accepted belief that Admiral Robert Peary was the first man to reach the North Pole was inaccurate, and the recognition finally went to his attendant Matthew Henson.*
Did you find the main idea _____ in the first sentences; ___✔___ in the last sentences; _____ in the middle of the paragraph; _____ was unstated, had to be inferred.
Supporting detail: *Admiral Robert Peary claimed he was the first man to reach the North Pole and return alive.*
Supporting detail: *Henson's family claimed Henson was the first to reach the North Pole.*
Supporting detail: *Inuit men who had been with them said Peary was ill and had to ride in a dogsled while Henson marched on and planted the American flag.*

Story 3:

Topic: testing rules
Main Idea: Most teenagers are abiding by new laws that ban the use of cell phones while driving. ✔
Did you find the main idea _____ in the first sentences; _____ in the last sentences; _____ in the middle of the paragraph; _____ was unstated, had to be inferred.

Supporting detail: Only certain types of calculators may be used and only during the math sections.
Supporting detail: Cell phones must be turned off and put away.
Supporting detail: Keep your eyes on your own paper.

Story 4:

Topic: getting older
Main Idea: Life can be enriching as we get older.
Did you find the main idea _____ in the first sentences; _____ in the last sentences; _____ in the middle of the paragraph; ✔ was unstated, had to be inferred.

Supporting detail: Many older people have successful lives.
Supporting detail: Many older people feel more self-confident.
Supporting detail: Those who are curious, read, learn new things, and exercise can even improve their minds.

Story 5:

Topic: pets
Main Idea: Some pets are used therapeutically to help people in many difficult circumstances.
Did you find the main idea _____ in the first sentences; ✔ in the last sentences; _____ in the middle of the paragraph; _____ was unstated, had to be inferred.

Supporting detail: Some pets can calm violent prisoners.
Supporting detail: Some pets can raise the moods, lessen depression and loneliness of senior citizens.
Supporting detail: Some pets are used to assist people with physical and mental disabilities.

Story 6:

Topic: changes in people
Main Idea: So, the truth that while some changes might be overnight wonders, most are long-term works in progress.
Did you find the main idea _____ in the first sentences; ____✔____ in the last sentences; _____ in the middle of the paragraph; _____ was unstated, had to be inferred.
Supporting detail: It took eons before humans walked upright, shed their thick hair, and could communicate using sounds.
Supporting detail: Genes play an important role in human change.
Supporting detail: It takes many years for these changes to become noticeable.

Story 7:

Topic: cooking
Main Idea: Following the right steps can turn a boring or inedible meal into a gourmet experience.
Did you find the main idea _____ in the first sentences; _____ in the last sentences; ____✔____ in the middle of the paragraph; _____ was unstated, had to be inferred.
Supporting detail: Cooking a great meal begins with a good recipe and ingredients and supplies.
Supporting detail: The recipes, supplies and ingredients can be found places.
Supporting detail: After deciding what to cook, you need to have everything nearby, ready to chop, measure, and cook.

Story 8:

Topic: student volunteering
Main Idea: (Implied) Students have different opinions about volunteering.
Did you find the main idea _____ in the first sentences; _____ in the last sentences; _____ in the middle of the paragraph; ____✔____ was unstated, had to be inferred.
Supporting detail: A growing number of schools require students to volunteer.
Supporting detail: Many students enjoy the experience.
Supporting detail: Other students feel it is an unfair requirement.

Page 85 **Identifying Signals in Reading Selections**

    1 or 7 a.

    10 b.

    8 c.

    1 or 7 d.

    3 e.

    4 or 6 f.

    5 g.

    4 or 6 h.

    2 i.

    9 j.

Page 85 **Hunters and Gatherers**

All people of long ago had to get food and shelter, just as we do today. **However,** we go to the store to buy our food; ancient populations had to rely on the land.

One way that people got their food was to walk around the area picking what grew wild on trees and bushes **such as** nuts and berries. **Another** way was to eat plants and roots that could be dug up. Both of these methods are called *gathering.*

While gathering could supply vegetables, nuts and fruits, humans **also** ate meat. **Therefore**, the cavemen learned to hunt animals **such as** deer and rabbits.

Most cavemen got their food by using both methods. They are **now** known as hunters and gatherers. This was their way of life, **or** their culture. Tools must also be devised to maintain that culture. **For example**, early people invented tools that allowed them to dig up plants more easily, and weapons that allowed them to kill more effectively. **As a result** of their inventiveness, the early human populations survived and the **most** skilled were able to spread their cultures throughout our world.

Page 93 **Steve Jobs**

Study Questions

1. Stephen Wozniak

2. He thought his parents were spending too much money.

3. He learned to recognize and appreciate the effort to create beauty, which led to his demanding beautiful design and fonts.

4. Mouse

5. After Pixar was sold to Disney Corporation

6. He got it at Hewlett after calling its co-founder/owner, William Hewett for some parts.

7. Answers will vary, but the gist is that people should always try to innovate and take risks but also enjoy life.

Page 95 **Volcanoes**

Study Questions:

1. What causes volcanoes to erupt?
   a. As the magma rises, gases are released that may cause an explosion that expels the magma through the earth's surface.

2. What is the "ring of fire?"
   b. The Pacific Plate in Japan, Alaska, Central America, South America and Indonesia form a circle on the global map, and together they are known as the "Ring of Fire."

3. Why do volcanoes exist only in some areas?
   a. They exist only near the edges of tectonic plates which have cracks.

4. What is the difference between magma and lava?
   a. Magma is molten rock within the Earth's crust. When magma erupts, it is called lava.

5. Do you think that Mount St. Helens has the potential to grow taller than Mauna Loa? Explain the reasons for your answer.
   a. Answers can vary, but the gist of it is that active volcanoes can continue to grow and Mount St. Helens is still an active volcano.

NOTE TAKING

Summarizing Activity:

Page 104 **Ice**

Topic: Ice
Main Idea: Ice is a mineral that freezes and has many interesting properties.
Supporting details: 1. Ice is a crystalline inorganic solid and is considered a mineral. 2. The physical properties of water and ice are controlled by a weak formation of hydrogen bonds between adjacent oxygen atoms. 3. Water expands when it freezes, so ice is actually lighter than water and has a gravity that is less than water's. Therefore, unlike other liquids that freeze, ice floats. 4. Water freezes at 32 degrees Fahrenheit, but if you add an impurity, such as salt, the freezing point lowers. 5. Ice melts under pressure so skaters actually skate on water.
Summary: Ice is a mineral whose physical properties are controlled by weak formations of hydrogen bonds between adjacent oxygen atoms. Because ice is lighter than water, unlike other frozen liquids, it floats. Though ice freezes at 32 degrees, impurities cause it to freeze at lower temperatures.

Page 107 Simple Outlining Exercise

Title

Pompeii, the City That Slept for 1,500 Years

I. Heading/Topic
Eruption

  A. Main idea
Citizens unaware of potential for disaster

    1. Supporting detail
Built upon the hardened lava from past volcanic eruption of Mt. Vesuvius in Italy

    2. Supporting detail
Built mansions, traded and enjoyed lives

  B. Main idea
79 A.D. Mount Vesuvius erupts

    1. Supporting detail
Loud explosion

    2. Supporting detail
Lava cascaded onto homes

    3. Supporting detail
Ash and pumice stone covered city

    4. Supporting detail
Electrical storm that blocked out daylight

    5. Supporting detail
Gaseous fumes killed remaining life

    6. Supporting detail
Rain hardens lava and buries city under 18 feet of crust

II. Heading/Topic

Discovery

  A. Main idea
Preservation most remarkable of its time

    1. Supporting detail
Hermetically sealed > 1,500 years

    2. Supporting detail
Remains of 2,000 people near-perfect condition

B. Main idea
Evidence found that people were surprised by eruption

    1. Supporting detail
    Food found

        a) Sub-detail
        eggs unbroken

        b) Sub-detail
        wine still drinkable

        c) Sub-detail
        food on table uneaten

    2. Supporting detail
    people in stages of action

        a) Sub-detail
        mother & daughter in embrace

        b) Sub-detail
        man defending gold

III. Heading/Topic
City Now Alive

A. Main idea
Pompei is bustling city

    1. Supporting detail
    3/5 ruins excavated

    2. Supporting detail
    Millions of visitors come

B. Main idea
This wouldn't go uncovered again

    1. Supporting detail
    People live on Mt. Vesuvious again

    2. Supporting detail
    Aware another eruption could happen

Page 112 **Mind Mapping the Brain**

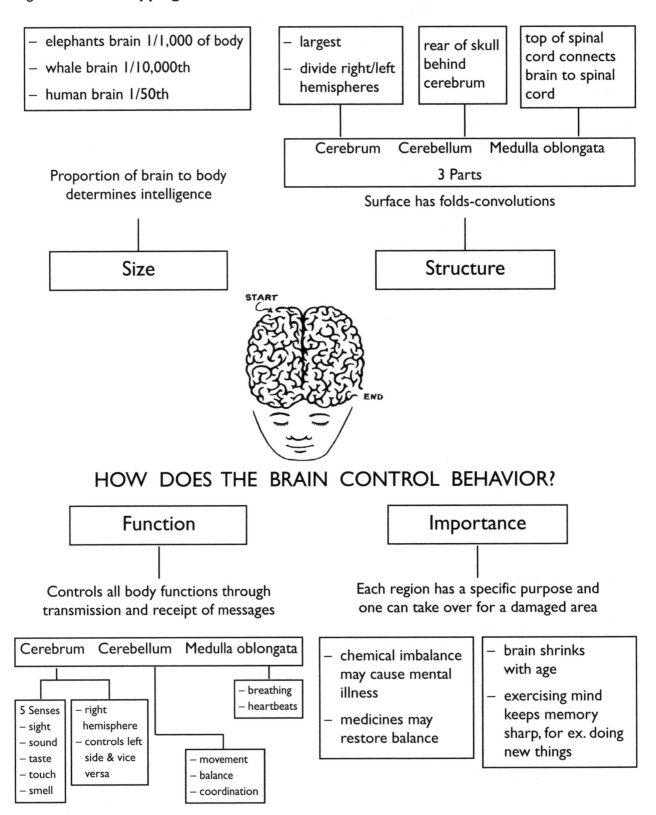

- elephants brain 1/1,000 of body
- whale brain 1/10,000th
- human brain 1/50th

- largest
- divide right/left hemispheres

rear of skull behind cerebrum

top of spinal cord connects brain to spinal cord

Cerebrum   Cerebellum   Medulla oblongata
3 Parts

Surface has folds-convolutions

Proportion of brain to body determines intelligence

Size

Structure

START

END

HOW DOES THE BRAIN CONTROL BEHAVIOR?

Function

Importance

Controls all body functions through transmission and receipt of messages

Each region has a specific purpose and one can take over for a damaged area

Cerebrum   Cerebellum   Medulla oblongata

5 Senses
- sight
- sound
- taste
- touch
- smell

- right hemisphere
- controls left side & vice versa

- breathing
- heartbeats

- movement
- balance
- coordination

- chemical imbalance may cause mental illness
- medicines may restore balance

- brain shrinks with age
- exercising mind keeps memory sharp, for ex. doing new things

Page 114 **Combo Notes:**

> **Henry VIII**

> **Henry VIII's private life changes English religious history**

> **Henry seeks to divorce first wife Catherine of Aragon**

★ Reasons
- ✗ Catherine produced no male heir
- ✗ Wanted to marry Anne Boleyn
- ✗ Should never been allowed to marry his brother's widow

★ Obstacles
- ✗ Still married to Catherine
- ✗ Catholic, so no divorces allowed
- ✗ Pope refused to annul marriage

★ Solutions
- ✗ Declares Pope has no authority in England
- ✗ Appoints Cranmer Archbishop of Canterbury
  - ✔ annuls Henry's marriage
  - ✔ declares Henry's marriage to Anne as legal

> **Parliament passes Act of Separation**

★ Finalizes England's break from Church of Rome
★ Establishes Anglican Church as official Church of England
- ✔ Names Henry head of Church of England
- ✔ Church allows divorces

> **Henry's six wives and what happened to them**

1. Catherine of Aragon
   - ★ marriage annulled
2. Anne Boleyn
   - ★ had a baby girl
   - ★ charged with infidelity, then beheaded
3. Jane Seymour
   - ★ produced male heir, then died while still married to Henry
4. Anne of Cleves
   - ★ marriage annulled
5. Catherine Howard
   - ★ accused of adultery, then beheaded
6. Catherine Paar
   - ★ outlived Henry

TEST TAKING ACTIVITIES

Summarizing Activity:

Page 143 Matching

1. E
2. A
3. H
4. C
5. [The ringer]
6. B
7. G
8. D
9. F

Page 143 Fill-In

1. equilateral
2. greater than 90 and less than 180
3. ½ (b X h)
4. trapezoid
5. octagon
6. circumference
7. parallel
8. intersect
9. perpendicular
10. isosceles

Page 144 True-False

1. F
2. T
3. F
4. F
5. F
6. T
7. F
8. F
9. T
10. F

Page 145 Multiple Choice

1. d
2. a
3. c
4. c
5. d
6. a
7. c
8. e
9. b
10. c

Page 146 Recall what you've learned about objective tests

1. e
2. c
3. e
4. a
5. e
6. directions
7. entire
8. recall questions
9. four
10. guess
11. T
12. F
13. T
14. T
15. F
16. b
17. d
18. a
19. c
20. e

Page 151 Activity: Apply what you've learned about tests

The First 10 U.S. Presidents

1. c
2. b
3. c
4. d
5. C
6. E
7. F
8. B
9. A
10. G
11. John Quincy Adams
12. James Madison
13. John Adams
14. William Henry Harrison
15. George Washington
16. F
17. F
18. T
19. F
20. T

Essay

Similarities:

Both signed the Declaration of Independence

Though political opponents, both served together as president (Adams) and vice-president (Jefferson)

Both died on the same day: July 4, 1826

Differences:

They were political opponents from different political parties.

Adams supported urban big business and national banking.

Jefferson supported farming and small business and opposed a national bank.